UNDERSTANDING

EQUINE
HOOF CARE

YOUR **GUIDE** TO HORSE HEALTH
CARE AND MANAGEMENT

ISBN-13: 978-1-58150-136-0
ISBN-10: 1-58150-136-6

Library of Congress Control Number: 2005933949

Printed in the United States of America
First Edition: 2006

UNDERSTANDING

EQUINE HOOF CARE

YOUR **GUIDE** TO HORSE HEALTH
CARE AND MANAGEMENT

By Heather Smith Thomas

Blood-Horse Publications, Lexington, KY

Other titles offered by
***The Horse* Health Care Library**

Understanding EPM (Revised)

Understanding Equine Lameness

Understanding Equine First Aid

Understanding the Equine Foot

Understanding Equine Nutrition

Understanding Laminitis

Understanding the Foal

Understanding the Broodmare

Understanding Basic Horse Care

Understanding the Stallion

Understanding Horse Behavior

Understanding Breeding Management

Understanding the Older Horse

Understanding Equine Law

Understanding the Young Horse

Understanding the Equine Eye

Understanding the Pony

Understanding Equine Neurological Disorders

Understanding Equine Business Basics

Understanding Equine Medications

Understanding Equine Acupuncture

Understanding Equine Preventive Medicine

Understanding Equine Colic

Understanding Your Horse's Behavior

The New Equine Sports Therapy

Horse Theft Prevention Handbook

Contents

INTRODUCTION

R egular hoof care is one of the most important facets of horse maintenance. The horse's hooves grow continuously to compensate for wear. If a horse does not have a chance to wear his feet down at the same rate they grow, hooves grow too long.

Wild horses' feet do not become too long because these animals travel constantly — wandering to graze and trekking to water — on relatively dry ground. Even on rocky ground wild horses rarely wear their feet down to the quick. Exceptions are those horses that must travel excessively during drought to find food or water; on occasion they wear their feet to the point of lameness or death.

When our ancestors domesticated horses, these animals had to adapt to hard roads, hard work, and less-than-perfect accommodations. They were brought from clean, dry prairies to confined housing or small pens that might be muddy part of the year. The fact that horses were often shod, combined with their living in an environment imposed by humans, led to the elimination of natural hoof wear.

When a horse's feet cannot wear normally, the hooves can become overlong and subject to cracking and breaking. Also, feet that have become too long put more strain on bones, tendons, ligaments, and joints, causing crooked legs or lameness.

However, if feet wear too much from excessive use, the horse loses the protective outer covering of the hoof and becomes lame from walking on the sensitive structures of the foot. Thus, for most domestic horses, shoes have become a necessity. The tribes of people who first tamed and used the horse for their own purposes discovered early on that a horse ridden regularly or strenuously needed foot protection.

The first devices for hoof protection (leather socks and straw sandals attached with thongs) were created thousands of years ago, before the Romans came up with the idea of making bronze shoes. The first metal shoes were laced on with leather straps, but it wasn't long before an innovative blacksmith discovered the outer hoof wall held no living tissues and began using nails.

Until quite recently, shoeing practices had not changed very much. Research and innovations in the past 40 years have given us more knowledge about hoof health, function, and disease — and new materials and methods for dealing with hoof problems. Medical research, gait and locomotion studies, and new techniques have provided farriers help for foot problems that used to be considered hopeless. This learning process is ongoing.

This book will help you understand the normal functions of the equine hoof and the basics of proper foot care. As most domestic horses do not have ideal conditions for normal hoof wear — either needing protection from excessive wear in the form of shoes or needing regular trimming because the feet do not get enough wear — the following chapters will also cover the basics of trimming and shoeing.

CHAPTER 1

Hoof Structure and Foot Facts

Knowing the anatomy and function of the foot can help you take better care of your horse's feet — and do a better job of trimming or shoeing if you do that yourself. A working knowledge of the foot also enables you to select animals with the most desirable structure. You want a horse that is more apt to stay sound through a long life of hard work.

The old saying, "No hoof, no horse" is very true, especially as it pertains to the horse's working ability and soundness. The horse is an athlete; we use him for a variety of athletic purposes — racing, jumping, chasing cattle, pulling carts. The health and soundness of his feet are of vital importance. Another old saying is that a horse is as old as his feet and legs. If they are not sound and healthy, he cannot be used for much.

It has also been said that a horse's feet and disposition both deteriorate when a horse is not used. His feet — and his mental and social nature — evolved with continual activity. Therefore, regular exercise is crucial. Because horses are creatures of movement, they are healthiest and happiest when they have room to roam, grazing on the go.

Horses are all unique. From head to hoof, each horse is genetically engineered to be built a little differently. Each horse's hooves have their own shape, hardness, and rate of growth. White (non-pigmented) hooves are often less resilient than colored ones. White hooves are softer when wet and more brittle when dry, making them more prone to chipping and cracking. As a result, white feet usually wear more quickly than pigmented ones. Some horses with white feet have tough hooves, but as a general rule when a horse has white feet and colored feet, the white ones are less resilient than the dark ones.

> # AT A GLANCE
>
> • Conformation and breed dictate a horse's foot type.
>
> • White feet tend to be less resilient.
>
> • Well-conformed feet withstand the damage caused by concussion and help keep a horse sound.
>
> • Climate plays a big role in the quality of a horse's feet.

In addition to genetics, climate also makes a difference; a moist environment makes hooves softer while dry conditions make hooves harder and tougher.

Breed difference is also a factor. Draft horses tend to have relatively flat feet. Their ancestors evolved in marshy regions of northern Europe — where a large, flat hoof was well suited for boggy ground, enabling a heavy horse to travel without sinking so deeply. Concussion was minimal on soft surfaces, so having a flat hoof didn't matter. At the other extreme, Arabian horses evolved in dry desert country. Their feet are smaller, blockier, and tougher, with a concave sole to prevent bruising. This type of sole has more flex and "give" to dissipate concussion; the sole can flatten as the hoof hits hard ground, then spring back into place when picked up.

ANATOMY OF THE FOOT

A horse's front leg from the knee down is like an elongated version of a human hand with most of the fingers missing. While the cannon bone is the equivalent of the middle bone in the human hand, the foot is similar to the end of a human finger. The pastern is the middle finger — with the long pastern bone, short pastern bone, and coffin bone (inside the hoof) being the three segments of the finger. The hoof is the fingernail — made of the same basic material, keratin (a type of simple protein that forms hair, skin, and horny tissues).

This specialized horny shell covers sensitive inner tissues, protecting bones, nerves, blood vessels, and tendons. The hoof wall grows continuously to make up for normal wear and broken edges, growing down from the corium of the coronary band at the hairline.

Just beneath the coronary band is the periople, a narrow strip similar to the cuticle on a human fingernail. It produces a waxy, varnish-like substance that covers the outer surface of the hoof wall to help seal it from the elements and prevent excessive drying. The outer surface (stratum tectorium) of the hoof wall itself also helps hold in moisture. When footing is soft and wet, the hoof becomes softer. When ground is dry and hard, the hoof dries out and becomes harder so it won't wear away too quickly. The healthy hoof adapts to environmental conditions but does not become too dry and brittle in dry weather.

The hoof wall is made up of tiny hollow tubes bundled tightly together — running from the coronary band to the ground surface of the foot. These tubules give some elasticity to the wall, helping it compress and expand without splitting. They carry and hold some moisture but have no blood supply. On the inner surface of the hoof wall, these tiny columns of tissue interface with the sensitive laminae that do contain blood and nerve endings.

The surface of the coffin bone is covered with soft "leaves" of velvet-like blood-filled tissue — the sensitive laminae — that hook into the tiny fingers of insensitive laminae inside the horny outer shell of the foot.

The coffin bone (the third phalanx or "end" finger bone) is suspended within the hoof capsule by the laminae. If this attachment is disrupted by inflammation (laminitis), the interface may come apart and allow the coffin bone to drop at the front or sink within the hoof, creating a condition called founder. Founder is the term describing the sequel to chronic laminitis, in which the coffin bone rotates or drops.

The tough, outer covering of the hoof consists of the wall, bars, frog, and sole. The bars, when looked at from the bottom of the foot, are seen as inward continuations of the hoof wall, serving as braces to keep the heels from contracting. The bars are an inward extension (between the sole and the frog on the ground-bearing surface of the foot) of the hoof wall at the heels. The V-shaped frog acts as a cushion in the middle of the sole; it helps absorb concussion and also regulates hoof moisture. The rear portion of the hoof wall (from the midpoint between toe and heel, where the wall makes a bend) is the quarter.

The region where sole and hoof wall meet is the white line. This junction is obvious on a freshly trimmed foot — yellowish at the sole edge and whiter toward the hoof wall side. The

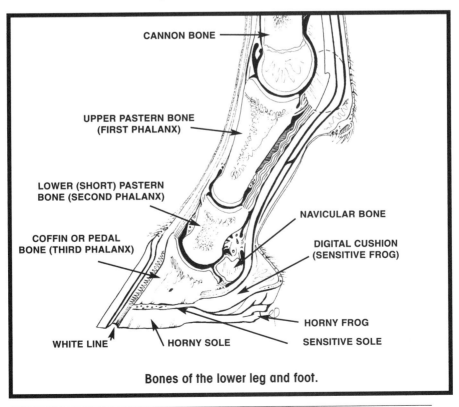

Bones of the lower leg and foot.

white line should be of uniform width all around the sole and, preferably, wide (about 3 mm). A wide white line indicates the hoof has strength and density; a thin line (especially if it has points of separation or a tendency to flake apart) may indicate weakness. If a white line is too wide, however, you may start seeing some separation.

The horny tissue outside the white line is insensitive horn, and everything inside the white line is "alive." Between the ground surface and coronary band, this white line region is the area where the insensitive laminae (tubular "fingers") from the horny outer tissues interlock with the sensitive laminae from the living tissues inside the hoof. The area at the bottom (ground surface) where the two types of laminae meet at the white line has some elasticity, creating a somewhat flexible link between the solid hoof wall and the softer sole. This elasticity also helps absorb shock when the foot contacts the ground, especially aiding in the expansion and contraction of the rear portions of the foot.

The hoof wall carries most of the weight when the foot is on the ground — especially when the horse is shod — and the bars act as wedges to help prevent over-expansion and contraction of the foot. The sole should be somewhat concave, especially on a riding horse, to give more grip on the ground and allow for expansion when weight is placed on the foot. If the sole is too flat or the walls have worn down so much that the horse is bearing weight on the sole, he may bruise his foot and become lame (unless he has toughened the sole running

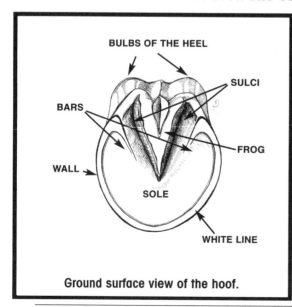

BULBS OF THE HEEL

SULCI

BARS

FROG

WALL

SOLE

WHITE LINE

Ground surface view of the hoof.

barefoot on hard ground). Front feet are usually rounder, larger, and stronger than hind feet because the horse's front legs support nearly two-thirds of his weight and are subjected to more wear and concussion.

The digital cushion (sometimes called the sensitive frog) is a blood-filled pad of connective tissue at the rear of the foot — lying above the frog and below and behind the coffin bone and navicular bone. This pad is the major shock absorption mechanism in the foot, using hydraulics to dissipate concussion. The digital cushion protects the bones as weight is placed on the foot, spreading apart as it is squeezed between the bones and the frog — an action that also forces the blood within it to go back up the leg. When the foot is lifted, the elastic tissue springs back to its original shape.

IMPORTANCE OF GOOD CONFORMATION

A hoof's conformation plays a role in its ability to hold up under long, heavy use. Genetics and nutrition are contributing factors in hoof structure (conformation) and in soundness. Soundness is influenced by conformation and circumstance (accidents).

Feet should be well shaped and proportionate to the size and weight of the horse. He needs enough hoof to support his body, but his feet should not be so large that they make him clumsy. If the feet are too small for his body structure, the horse will not hold up under strenuous use. The increased shock of concussion in a small hoof area can lead to laminitis or to heel pain. It can also lead to other problems that are all too often lumped together as "navicular disease" and to joint problems in the leg (due to excessive concussion traveling up the leg from the foot).

The navicular bone, located behind and underneath the coffin bone, serves as a fulcrum to give the deep flexor tendon more support and leverage. The navicular bursa is the small lubricating sac surrounding the navicular bone; it cushions the tendon that glides over the bone. If the navicular bone or bursa suffers excessive trauma or concussion (the incidence of which is increased with poor conformation), the horse may become lame. In some breeds, selective breeding for looks rather than function has resulted in many individuals with feet too small for their body weight. This, in turn, has led to increased incidence of unsoundness.

Hooves should be wide at the heels, so the heels can "give" and spring apart when the foot hits the ground. This flexibility helps absorb and dissipate some of the concussion. Otherwise, all the jarring would be transmitted directly to the bones of the foot, leg, and joints — making them more vulnerable to concussion-related injuries. The foot should be fairly deep at the heel, not shallow and close to the ground. A strong, deep heel is less apt to bruise and also has thicker, stronger bars.

The sole should be almost round, very thick (less easily bruised), and should shed normally; the old sole continually flakes off as new sole grows — there is no abnormal buildup of dead sole material. Soles should be slightly concave in the front feet and more concave in the hind feet. Flat feet put a horse at risk for stone bruising. The navicular bone, located just above

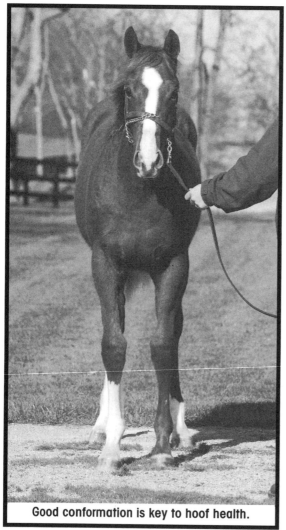

Good conformation is key to hoof health.

the center of the frog, is more at risk for concussion trauma in a flat-footed horse. The frog should be large and healthy, cen-tered in the sole and pointing to the toe of the foot, with definite grooves (sulci) on each side and a groove or cleft down its center.

The hoof wall should be fairly thick, pliable, and resistant to drying out. The thickest, hardest,

and toughest hoof horn is at the toe. Under natural conditions (barefoot) the toe suffers more wear than the rest of the hoof wall due to breakover when the horse picks up his foot. The toe also gets wear because it helps pull the horse along at all gaits, digging into the ground as it breaks over.

If a horse has good foot and leg conformation, his hooves usually wear evenly because the foot breaks over the center of the toe. He won't wear one side of the foot more than the other, nor dub (wear) off one side of the toe. To a great extent, leg conformation determines the shape of the feet — because of the way they are picked up, swung through the air, and set down on the ground. Leg structure determines whether feet are picked up squarely and land squarely or start and end their flight crookedly. A horse with crooked legs and poor joint angles will have unbalanced feet that wear crookedly; one side of the foot will be a different shape than the other, and the frog will usually be pointed off center.

If the frog is off center, there's often a flare in the hoof wall on one side instead of a symmetrical ground surface — one side of the foot receives more impact than the other. The side with more impact is steeper because the rate of hoof growth on that side speeds up due to increased circulation. The side receiving less impact will flare outward. If one side of the foot continually hits the ground harder than the other, the heel bulb on the hard-impact side may eventually be driven upward, creating a condition called sheared heels. This may result in lameness. If the horse lands on one side of the foot and breaks over on that side rather than straight, that side will be worn more than the other side, even if the hoof wall is straighter and the other side is flared.

The coronary band should be perfectly symmetrical. The hairline at the top of the hoof should be smooth and straight and not distorted. If the foot gets more impact on one side than the other, the coronary band will give a clue; it will be driven upward in that area, making an uneven hair line.

A dished appearance at the front of the foot may be due to lack of circulation in the toe area or due to forces created when the toe is too long. Long toes increase the leverage force in the foot and may cause tearing of the laminae. A dished toe can also be the result of chronic laminitis. The front of the foot is no longer a line, but curved, tending to curl up at the toe.

CONCUSSION FACTORS

Concussion — the jarring and impact as the horse's feet hit the ground while traveling — is one of the major causes of lameness. The trauma of hitting hard surfaces at high speeds creates stress on hoof structures and on the bones and joints up the leg.

The horse's foot is remarkably well made for counteracting the effects of concussion, but it works best when the foot is of proper size and shape, with strong, deep heels. The digital cushion above the frog and heels can be compressed, expanding outward, pushing the elastic cartilage outward and back as the foot takes weight. The concave sole flattens a little and descends as weight is put on it, with all structures working together to help push venous blood back up the leg as well as dissipating the concussion. The more nearly ideal the foot and leg conformation, the more uniformly the stresses are distributed. However, poor conformation puts added stress on the legs and hooves and — aggravated by concussion — may eventually lead to lameness and unsoundness.

As a horse walks, the foot's pumping action and the fetlock joint's spring absorb most of the shock in the leg. The foot expands as it takes weight, and the digital cushion acts as a buffer between the foot bones and the weight-bearing frog. The coffin joint, between the coffin bone and the short pastern bone, has some move-ment and elas-ticity because of the way the navicular bone is placed (with its pulley action for the flexor tendon). Direct concussion to the coffin joint is avoided by transferring

Concussion can cause lameness.

some of the weight from the short pastern bone above it to the navicular bone — which is well supported by the deep flexor tendon behind and below it.

HOOF GROWTH

The hoof wall grows about 1/4- to 3/8-inch per month; the entire hoof wall should be replaced by new horn every eight to 12 months though some horses have a slower or faster rate of hoof growth. If a horse is shod, his shoes need to be reset or replaced (after proper hoof trimming) every four to 14 weeks, with six to 10 weeks being average — de-pending on rate of hoof growth and whether the feet are balanced. If a horse's feet grow fast and the foot is out of balance, the toes may become too long in just three to four weeks after shoeing, with more risk for stumbling. Other in-dividuals can easily go two months or longer (especially if the feet are balanced) before needing to be shod again —

unless the shoes wear out faster.

The hoof wall grows downward from the coronary band; any injury to this band will affect hoof growth in that area. The normal wall is smooth, with no rings, bumps, or ridges. Rings and ripples are signs of uneven hoof growth. The horse may have experienced nutritional stress, illness, or some other stress during the time that part of the hoof wall was growing down from the coronary band.

An inflamed coronary band or severe fever will produce thicker (but not healthier) horn that results in a ridge. A nutritional deficiency or lack of circulation to the horn-growing tissue may produce thinner horn, which grows out as a groove. A single ring on all four feet at the same location may be the aftereffect of a serious illness. A fever may temporarily alter hoof growth. Ripples may indicate a mild case of laminitis. Multiple rings that are farther apart at the heel than at the toe show uneven growth from chronic laminitis (founder). Some rings can be caused by dietary changes or seasonal variations of hoof growth; for example, warm weather and green grass tend to make a hoof grow faster.

A single lump on a hoof is usually the result of local trauma. It may weaken the wall and lead to cracking, or the defect may just move down the wall as the hoof grows — until worn or trimmed away.

The horny sole continuously grows downward from the sensitive inner sole above it; little cracks develop in the old sole and help it flake away. The outer layer is dead tissue. This self-trimming process is called exfoliation. A horse's sole generally needs no trimming when the foot is trimmed. Trimming a normal sole may intrude into sensitive tissues and make the horse tenderfooted or lame. Occasionally, however, dead material on the sole builds up — especially if the horse is kept in a muddy environment where the sole never dries out. The extra material must be carefully trimmed away with a hoof knife to the proper level. Otherwise, the hoof wall cannot be trimmed adequately, and the layer of dead sole may continue to build up and provide a place for bacterial growth.

THE FROG

In unshod horses the bottom of the hoof wall, the frog, and bars of the foot are all level and flat to the ground, and each helps bear the weight of the horse. On soft surfaces or if dirt packs in, the sole also bears weight. The bars and frog have less contact with the ground on a shod horse unless footing is soft or uneven — such as rocks and gravel — because shoes put a hoof a 1/4-inch or more above the ground. On perfectly flat ground, shoeing hinders the ability of the bars and frog to take some of the weight.

The horse's ancestors roamed grassy prairies and could run barefoot all their lives without becoming tenderfooted. But horses ridden in rocky terrain usually need shoes to keep from wearing down the feet too fast (eventually getting down to the quick because growth can't keep up with wear) and to avoid lameness from stone bruising. If frogs and bars are left flat with the ground, the horse would soon go lame. In rocky terrain these structures are more protected if they are a fraction of an inch off the ground.

The frog is the softest part of the hoof, made of the same fibrous material as the rest of the external hoof except it contains oil glands. Thus, it is more rubbery and usually contains more water. In moist conditions the frog is 50 percent water, by weight. In dry seasons it becomes smaller and more shriveled.

The frog, being somewhat soft and flexible, functions as a shock absorber, directing concussion outward instead of up the leg when the foot hits the ground. The softer frog complements the rigidity of the rest of the foot, allowing the hoof to have some give — to counteract the shock and concussion of landing on hard surfaces. The open heel and wedge-shaped frog allow the hoof to expand and contract as weight is placed on it and then released. The frog also provides more traction for the ground surface of the foot.

Horses that live in soft, wet pastures tend to have bigger, softer frogs than horses in dry or rocky terrain. Wet, swampy footing tends to make the whole hoof expand and flatten out, and the frog is always in contact with the ground because the foot sinks into the soft footing. A horse living in dry country develops harder and more upright hoof walls, pulling the frog up off the ground and getting it up out of the way of sharp rocks.

The "pancake" feet of many draft horses (breeds that developed in moist climates of Europe and the British Isles) were needed for keeping such large animals from sinking into soft ground, spreading the weight over a larger area. These horses have large frogs that have complete contact with the ground. The opposite extreme is the desert animal such as the donkey or burro, which has a narrow, upright, contracted foot and a frog so high that it never hits the ground. Some zebras have no frog at all.

Most riding horses fall between these two extremes, with hooves and frogs that can adapt to different conditions. Feral horses (domestic horses of various breeds gone wild) on dry western rangelands usually have feet so hard they can travel reasonable distances in rocks without becoming sore and tender; their frogs are small, dry, and usually off ground level so they won't be cut and bruised.

The Frog Pressure Debate

Farriers have had many arguments over the years as to proper care of frogs. Traditional wisdom that had its roots in horse care and farriery from the British and European experience (in a predominantly moist climate with deep soils) insists that frog pressure (flattening the frog to the ground) is crucial to hoof health, that the frog should never be trimmed at all, and that a hoof in which the frog doesn't touch the ground is an unhealthy hoof. This is true if the horse is on soft footing. Yet in horses that must traverse rocky terrain, constant frog contact with the ground can be disastrous. The logical answer to the frog pressure debate is that everything is relative, depending on what the environmental conditions are and what is expected of the foot.

Nature's plan is for the foot to expand each time it takes weight, forcing the bars apart fully, pushing the digital cushion upward to exert a pumping action on the network of blood vessels inside the foot. All the blood inside this cushion enables it to act as a big sponge to absorb concussion. Weight pushing down on this "sponge" (and upward pressure from sole and frog) also aids circulation because blood flows easily down into the foot but needs a little help getting back up. In the upper leg, muscle action helps move blood back to the heart, but there are no muscles below the knee or hock. The hoof's actions help move the blood up out of the multitude of capillary beds in the foot; the internal structures of the horse's foot contain more blood than his brain.

Movement and travel keep venous blood pumping back up the leg and arterial blood rushing down to the hoof to replace it, keeping all the hoof tissues well supplied with oxygen and nutrients; the hoof is healthiest when a horse is moving around and least healthy when he's confined to a small space.

CHAPTER 2

The Natural Foot

Recent studies of wild and feral horses have shown that horses can do very well barefoot; their feet are strong and healthy. A growing number of farriers today are trying to trim and shoe horses in ways that more closely approximate the natural hoof.

The wild or feral horse has few of the hoof problems that plague domestic horses, partly because the feet of the free-roaming horse are doing the work they were designed for — carrying him over clean, dry ground with almost constant (but not excessive) activity. The wild horse has tough, thick, healthy hoof walls and soles. Yet, if he were subjected to the use given some of our domestic horses (those that are used hard daily, in rocky terrain, for instance), he too, would need shoes.

The art and science of shoeing have progressed in fits and starts since the first innovative horseman nailed shoes to the equine foot. Shoeing began as a crude but workable way to keep the hoof from wearing away too fast with hard use. This is still the main reason many horsemen put shoes on their horses — to protect the feet from excessive wear and tender-footedness.

As farriers learned more about the anatomy of the foot and ways to attach a shoe without crippling or hindering the horse, shoeing became the "norm" for the domestic horse. Farriery has come a long way from its infancy in the Middle Ages and has contributed much help in the challenge of keeping hard-working horses sound. There is still a lot to learn, however, and during the past two decades some farriers have taken a more scrutinizing look at the natural foot of wild and feral horses to help fine-tune their ideas and techniques for creating a healthier shod foot.

THE HORSE IN NATURE

During the 1980s a few farriers began looking at natural feet, intrigued by differences in the wild foot and the shod hoof. The wild and feral horses had much shorter toes; deeper, stronger heels; and no incidence of navicular disease. Les Emery's book *Horse Shoeing Theory and Hoof Care* addresses the idea that navicular problems might be solved by making a hoof more natural — by raising the heels and shortening the toe.

After reading that book and seeing the feet of a mustang mare, farrier Jaime Jackson went looking for more "wild" hooves to study, particularly high-heeled horses that were sound and free of navicular disease. What he found, however, was sound horses with short toes, a very different kind of hoof structure than any other he'd ever encountered as a farrier. From 1982 to 1984, he studied feral horse herds in several areas of the West, and he eventually wrote a book called *The Natural Horse*. In it he describes what he considers to be the basis for trimming and shoeing horses in order to have more natural hoof care, and he puts forth the idea that horses could go barefoot.

In 1995 Jackson met Hiltrud Strasser, a German veterinarian who, since 1980, had been exploring barefootedness as a way to treat various lamenesses. She had written a book, *Lifetime of Soundness*, and had founded a certification course for holistic hoof care providers who base their work on principles of the natural hoof. Jackson took an even more holistic approach to natural hoof care and wrote his second book, *Horse Owners Guide to Natural Hoof Care.* He abandoned his farriery to become what he called a natural hoof care provider. He thought many lamenesses in horses result from unbalancing the hoof and sealing it off with inflexible metal, impairing normal hoof mechanics.

Meanwhile, Tia Nelson, a farrier/veterinarian in Helena, Montana, began shoeing horses in 1980. By 1984 she was sure that farriers were doing something wrong. She was frustrated by the fact that unsound horses (which could not be helped much by shoeing methods) could do better if she took their shoes off and turned them out on 20,000 acres and let them run loose for three months. In 1988 she started looking at feral horses' feet and in 1989 began looking at domestic barefoot horses. She followed the latter for several years, trying to understand their feet and interpret what she was seeing into something that could be useful in trimming and shoeing. Like Jackson, she noticed that the barefoot horses' toes were shorter and the hoof walls thicker and stronger than those of shod horses.

Nelson worked with about 25 horses — her own and some belonging to clients. Those 25 horses did very well barefoot, in hard use on rough ground. She found that horses ridden on decomposed granite (hard, dry, rocky soils) tend to do much better than horses kept in soft irrigated pastures. On dry ground, hooves are not so soft and do not wear away as fast.

When she started trimming and shoeing to mimic what feral horses' feet were doing, shortening the toe and bringing back the breakover and the heel, both the lame and sound horses she shod did better. Barrel racing horses started finishing their runs as much as three-quarters of a second faster. The horses could move faster and were not worried about their feet and footing.

When Nelson went to Colorado State University to become a veterinarian, she kept shoeing. Horses came to the university with sore heels, diagnosed with navicular disease, and were shod with egg bar shoes, wedge pads, and other traditional methods without a lot of success. So she started trimming these horses' feet back to the parameters of the feral and domestic barefoot horses, putting on a shoe that was square-toed and rolled, supporting the heels; the horses got better. They went back to competing in a short time.

About the same time (in 1986 and 1987) a Montana farrier, Gene Ovnicek, measured and imprinted hooves of 46 feral horses. These horses' hooves were consistent, with shapes and angles quite different from those usually seen in domestic horses. Later he worked with other farriers and several veterinarians at Colorado State University and at Michigan State University Veterinary School to study the anatomy, radiology (X-rays), and cell and tissue structures of feral horses' feet and compare them with domestic horses' feet.

One of the interesting findings was that the hoof wall of the wild horse usually makes only four points of contact with the ground when standing on a flat surface — at each heel and at both sides of the toe, making a square pattern of support. The toe itself is usually dubbed off (worn away), and the wall at the quarters is generally gone — not quite reaching the ground surface. This is the weakest part of the hoof wall on any hoof.

Because the hoof wall is usually worn away except at the heels and at the sides of the toe, the sole and frog may bear part of the weight if the hoof is packed with dirt. By contrast, the shod horse carries more weight on the hoof wall and laminae, even though the frog and sole tissues may be better suited for weight bearing because they are fatty and cushioning.

The toe of a free-roaming, barefoot horse is blunt and somewhat square, with breakover occurring at the center or close to it. The widest part of the foot is usually slightly in front of the point of the frog. The hoof wall at the toe does not have the destructive leverage forces that pull against a longer toe.

The wall at the quarters has no leverage forces — because there is no ground contact.

Breakover is the forward-most part of the foot in contact with the ground as the foot leaves the ground. A hoof with a short toe leaves the ground more quickly than a hoof with a long toe. The foot rotates over the breakover point as it begins to leave the ground. The force required to break over is greater with a long toe; there is a greater distance from the foot's center of gravity to the breakover point.

With the toe worn off, the hoof of a free-roaming horse has a relatively consistent breakover point about 1 to 1 1/2 inches in front of the tip of the frog (actual distance depends on the size of the foot). The shod domestic horse generally has a much longer toe, with the breakover point about 2 inches or more from the tip of the frog. Hoof length at the front on a wild or feral horse is rarely more than 3 inches (distance from coronary band to ground surface), whereas the domestic horse of same size and body weight often has a toe length of 3 1/2 inches or more, thereby creating a different foot angle. It also creates a different type of foot flight and forces the foot to land flat or toe first instead of heel first. Landing flat-footed creates more shock and trauma for the navicular bone, tendons, and coffin joint, which are more easily damaged.

The heel has more resilient tissues (digital cushion, hoof cartilage, and frog). These can absorb concussion much better than the other structures of the foot. In the domestic horse, however, these structures are often slightly atrophied because of improper trimming and shoeing.

FOUR-POINT TRIM

Some farriers are now using what they call the "four-point trim" to simulate what happens with natural hoof wear. This involves shortening the toe so the hoof is more naturally shaped — a bit blockier, without such a long toe. This helps many horses get "back under themselves" with more support to the leg and not so much strain on tendons from an overly long toe. This type of trimming has been done for a long time, but only in recent years, with the advent of feral horse foot studies, has it become more popular. The four-point trim can often help correct dished walls and grow out toe cracks and quarter cracks by removing the ground-bearing surfaces between the four supporting pillars of the hoof.

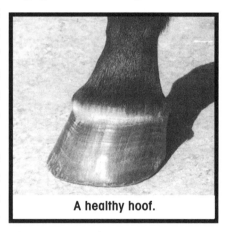

A healthy hoof.

When a problem foot is first trimmed this way, it looks vastly different from the symmetrical, circular foot that modern farriers look upon as ideal. Over time, however, it attains a structural integrity that enables it to maintain itself at or near ideal shape without having to continue the four-point trim. Until a foot can produce dense, tough horn, it is hard to balance it or have shoes stay on properly. Repeated shoeing of a hoof with a weak wall will often just make the weakness worse. Some farriers feel that the quickest and most effective way to correct certain types of problem feet is to let the horse go barefoot in the four-point trim for several months.

Mother Nature, without help from a farrier, can correct many "bad" feet if the horse can be turned out on dry ground for a year, with no trimming. On terrain where the foot can self-trim (get adequate wear), the hoof will remodel itself accordingly. Turnout on soft ground, however, or in small enclosures where the horse can't get enough exercise, will not accomplish this goal. The feet can't wear enough and will grow too long (putting strain on joints) and suffer hoof breakage.

For the shod athlete, the best foot is usually attained by keeping the toe short for proper breakover and foot angle but not removing support at the quarters. The free-roaming horse gets by without it — he's not using his feet as much —

but a horse competing in athletic activities carrying a rider needs that support.

HOOF ANGLES

When a horse is standing squarely, the slope of the hoof and the slope of the pastern should be the same. If the toe is too long and the heel too short, this angle line is broken toward the rear. If the toe is too short and the heels too long and high, the angle line is broken forward. For best agility, soundness, and hoof balance, the pastern and hoof must create an unbroken line — both at the same angle. If the horse is allowed to wear his feet naturally, these angles are usually the same.

The most commonly measured aspect of foot balance is toe angle. Long before farriers used hoof protractors to determine the exact angle of the hoof, someone decided that 45 degrees was the proper angle for a horse's front feet — the angle made between the ground surface and slope of the foot/pastern. Hind feet could be a little steeper, such as 52 to 55 degrees. This "ideal" hoof angle has been espoused by authors of books on conformation and shoeing for more than two centuries, but it is not correct for most horses. Under natural conditions, most horses have a more upright hoof, with the front foot angle closer to 55 degrees.

If a horse is allowed to run barefoot on large, dry pastures

A long toe puts excessive weight on the heels and can lead to soundness problems.

and wear his feet normally, he usually has a steeper hoof angle than the traditional "norm," since his toe is shorter. A sloping foot with a 45-degree angle makes the toe too long for many horses. It puts excessive weight on the heels and stress on the deep flexor tendon — and hence the navicular bone.

Indeed, overly long toes often create navicular problems. A horse's hoof angle should fit his individual conformation, which it will do if he is allowed to wear his feet normally.

For two centuries racehorse trainers had equated a long toe/low heel to a longer stride (due to delayed breakover), but in recent years this was proven false. The stride is not actually lengthened very much with a long toe. The long toe/low heel just puts more stress on the foot and leg, increases toe-first impact, and does more damage to the navicular bone. It's also been shown in several studies to be directly correlated to cata-strophic failure of the suspensory apparatus (tearing of the suspensory ligament, fractures of the sesamoid bones, etc.). For most horses, putting the foot out of balance to make an "ideal" 45-degree angle with a longer toe puts the entire leg structure out of whack. If we interfere with a horse's natural angles and balance, we create problems.

> ## AT A GLANCE
>
> A natural foot or four-point trim:
>
> • Puts the breakover point of the foot back farther.
>
> • Encourages heel length.
>
> • Decreases strain on the deep digital flexor tendon.
>
> • Increases the force and strength of the suspensory system in the lower leg.
>
> • Increases efficiency of movement.

Angles within a foot should be the same. Toe angle and heel angle should match. A mismatch creates an unbalanced and abnormal foot. The slope of the heel being greater than the slope of the toe, for instance, creates a condition called un-derslung (underrun) heels — an increase in hoof angle ratio. A clubfooted horse, on the other hand, has an abnormally upright foot.

Hoof angle ratio is a measure of the relative slope of the angle of the front of the hoof versus the back (heel). As the toe gets longer (more sloped) and the heel gets shorter (heel bulbs closer to the ground), the horse has more problems staying sound.

A study done a few years ago at Colorado State University

by Dr. C. Wayne McIlwraith looked at certain aspects of conformation in racing Thoroughbreds and Quarter Horses and how these correlated with racing injuries. Among his findings was that underslung heels and a long toe increase risks for knee injuries in the front legs and for fetlock joint injuries in the hind legs. For example, the CSU study found that when toe length increased by one inch, the odds of that horse's sustaining a chip fracture in the knee increased by a factor of 40.33.

In addition, McIlwraith's study found that the risk for hind fetlock injury increased 1.1 times for every degree of increase in front/back hoof angle in the hind feet. The risk for front leg (knee) injury increased 1.45 times for each 10 percent increase in front/back hoof angle in the front feet. Thus, improper hoof balance in the front feet increased the odds for knee swelling and front leg fractures. Other studies — at the University of California Davis — found that underrun heels also increase the risk for suspensory injuries.

NATURAL HOOF BALANCE

When Tia Nelson began shoeing horses with much shorter toes (and heels pulled back farther on the bottom of the foot), mimicking wild horse feet, she found the feet functioned just like wild horse feet with proper balance. Shortening the toe by backing the foot up and changing the hoof angle to approximate more closely the wild foot is much better than trying to shorten the toe by just trimming the bottom of the hoof wall.

Foot balance is crucial but not always understood. Terms like level, flat, and balanced are used as if interchangeable, but they are not. Balance should also not be confused with symmetry. Balance and symmetry are important in the foot, but they are not the same thing. Hoof balance is not static; it is three-dimensional and ever changing as the horse moves. It's balance in motion.

As Nelson describes it, a seesaw is balanced until you put a child on one end. If you don't change something to counterbalance the weight (either a child on the other end, or changing the length of the board or the placement of the fulcrum), it is no longer balanced. The hoof must

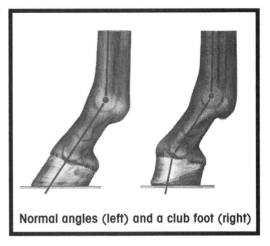

Normal angles (left) and a club foot (right)

also be able to change dynamically to accommodate instantly what happens when it takes weight and goes through the various phases of stride.

All the horses Nelson shoes get a custom shoeing job to suit each foot. More than 99 percent of the horses shod by Nelson get regular shoes out of a box. She sticks the shoe in a forge just to square and roll the toe, but the trimming (before the shoe is applied) is what is important to balance the foot. She uses a proportional guideline (which she calls the golden rectangle) to obtain proper hoof balance — a proportionality that works well on the hoof. The number involved is the Greek number phi (1.618). When she trims a hoof, she ends up with approximately 2/5 to 1/3 of the hoof ahead of Duckett's dot on the bottom of the frog and 3/5 to 2/3 of the hoof behind this dot.

Duckett's dot is an indentation near the apex of the frog. Once you identify this landmark, you can balance each foot for its best proportionality. When the frog is smoothed up and trimmed of loose tags, it's fairly easy to see this spot. On the average-sized hoof of a 1,000- to 1,200-pound horse, this spot is about 1/4- to 3/8-inch behind the apex of the prepared frog. From that point forward to the breakover point is about 2/5 to 1/3 of the bearing length of a balanced foot from front to back. Behind this dot (to the back of the foot) is 3/5 to 2/3 of the bearing length, or more than half.

If a horse's hooves are allowed to wear naturally, the breakover point is very close to where the foot ends (with its short toe and steeper foot angle). But if we put a shoe on, the breakover point is more forward, the toe will not be worn off, and the foot will be longer from front to back, creating a more sloped angle. The length from Duckett's dot to the breakover point will be too long (approaching half or more of the bearing surface) and the foot unbalanced.

The actual length from Duckett's dot to the breakover point varies with each horse. The steeper-angled horse with more upright hoof and pastern will have different measurements than a horse with less steep angles. How many inches ahead of the frog's tip the breakover point will be is also much different on a pony than on a Shire. And if you are shoeing an upright mule-type foot, it will be different than when you are shoeing a Thoroughbred.

A 1,200-pound Thoroughbred with a long shoulder and pastern angle should not be shod the same as a 1,200-pound Quarter Horse with upright shoulders and pasterns. The proportional difference between Duckett's dot and the breakover should be very different even though both horses are the same weight and may wear the same size shoe. Perfect proportionality for each horse is the golden rectangle ratio, since on many horses it is not exactly 1/3:2/3. It is a little off of 2/3 — which is closer to the golden rectangle used by Nelson. This seems to be the ideal for front feet.

Hind feet are totally different in shape but still have the 1/3: 2/3 parameters. The function is different than that of a front foot; hind feet are shaped for propulsion rather than navigation. Most horseshoers get the front/back balance correct on the hind feet. If there is a balance problem on the hind feet, it is usually side to side. The inside is often too upright and the outside flared. The upright side needs to be lowered and the flare taken off the outside, and you need to support the horse with just a tiny bit extra on the inside — so the foot can start sorting itself out to regain balance.

Nelson works on lame horses all over the country and when she brings feet back to proportionality, the horses become sound. Putting the hoof back into balance and proportionality works on foundered horses; navicular horses; and horses with ringbone, that stumble, or on those that just are a little off due to foot discomfort. Most of the traditional "corrective" shoeing done in the past was a quick fix that did not address the problem of hoof balance

If a foot is unbalanced side to side, one side is longer than the other and the hoof can't land evenly; the side that lands first bears the brunt of impact and is prone to injury — everything from bruised or sheared heels to quarter cracks. Mechanical stresses on the foot from the uneven weight bearing can lead to hoof wall separations, a problem that puts the hoof at risk for white line disease. Uneven landing also torques the leg above, putting bones, joints, and supportive structures at risk for injury as well. The load should be equal all around the foot, and this can only occur if feet are balanced and correct for that horse's conformation. If a foot is stressed, it is out of balance. If it's in balance, the forces acting on it are all equal. From a physics standpoint, if two things are pushing on an object and it's staying static in its environment, it is in balance.

The individual horse's leg conformation should dictate what is ideal for that horse — as Mother Nature would do if the horse were running free. Most horses' joint surfaces (on up the leg) are not perfectly symmetrical; the inside does not exactly match the outside. The inside of the limb generally carries slightly more of the weight, just because a horse's center of gravity is toward the midline of his body. Thus, the inside of the hoof is often slightly steeper (from coronary band to ground surface) than the outside wall. The latter is a little more sloped. If a horse naturally toes out slightly, his "normal" and best hoof balance includes a slightly non-symmetrical hoof wall. Studies at UC Davis found the majority of racing Thoroughbreds examined had an inner hoof wall

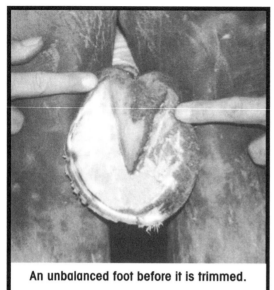

An unbalanced foot before it is trimmed.

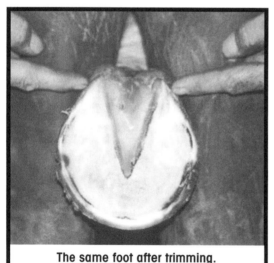

The same foot after trimming.

angle (front feet) of 77 degrees (more upright) and an outer wall angle of 73 degrees (more sloped). Leg conformation must always be taken into consideration when evaluating hoof balance.

SHOD OR BAREFOOT?

Some horsemen strongly believe the unshod hoof is healthier than a shod foot and just as capable of withstanding the stresses of riding and athletic competition that most people assume can only be handled with shoes.

A horse kept in a stall cannot keep his feet as hard and strong as a horse living in a 300-acre hillside pasture. A horse ridden daily in rocky country to move and gather cattle may eventually wear his feet too much (or stone bruise) even if he has strong, tough hooves. He will probably need shoes during the time of year he is used hard and steady. On the other hand, a horse being ridden regularly on ground that is less rocky may get by fine without shoes.

It is difficult to pattern a domestic horse's foot exactly on the feral or wild horse's foot; the domestic horse may carry 200 pounds of extra weight and may be asked to do much more than a wild horse does. Domestic horses are usually in an unnatural situation, being more confined. Feet don't get proper, natural exercise. The exercise is either too little (when the horse is not being ridden) or too much for the barefoot hoof to withstand (when the horse is being ridden hard). Unless a horse is pastured in a large area and it is the same kind of terrain over which you ride, the horse will not be in a natural circumstance when ridden barefoot.

> **AT A GLANCE**
>
> To determine if a horse can go barefoot, evaluate:
>
> - His hoof structure and strength.
>
> - How closely natural conditions can be simulated in his everyday environment.
>
> - The type of work performed.

It's nice if a horse can be kept barefoot, but shoeing for protection as when a horse must work on rocky ground or for a specialized task is reasonable — to enhance his ability to do his job.

A horse owner who decides against shoes must take other things into consideration. In order to keep the feet strong and healthy, the horse's lifestyle must be kept more natural, too. Barefoot won't work if he is still kept in an environment where his feet stay too soft or he cannot get steady, moderate exercise.

Trying to bring a horse that's been shod all his life back to a natural condition to let him go barefoot is sometimes a gradual process. At first the horse will be tenderfooted if he travels on rocks or gravel; there must be a transitional period as normal hoof function is restored. Some hooves are very distorted after being shod a long time and must be trimmed until proper balance can be re-established (being careful not to overdo what needs to be done, or it may cause the horse pain). A major factor in restoring hoof health in horses with foot problems is to change the horse's environment so he is never confined or standing around in a moist stall or muddy pen. The more nearly the domestic horse can approach natural conditions, the healthier his feet will be.

CHAPTER 3

Cleaning and Trimming Feet

Perhaps the single most important aspect of hoof care for the confined horse is regular cleaning and inspection. Horses kept in a stall or pen — where feet are in contact with manure and urine — should have their feet cared for daily. Horses should also have their feet inspected and cleaned before they are ridden. This regular handling of a horse's feet can accomplish two things: The horse comes to accept hoof care as part of his routine and becomes easier to trim or shoe, and his hoof health is constantly monitored and maintained.

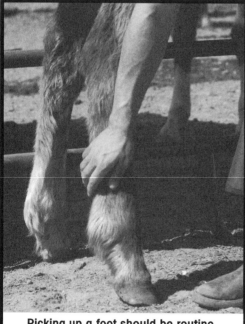

Picking up a foot should be routine.

FOOT HANDLING

To pick up a front foot, make sure the horse is comfortable so he can shift his weight easily off the leg you wish to pick up. If he is standing unevenly, don't try to pick up a leg he has a lot of weight on; make him change position first by leading him forward a step.

Stand beside the front leg, facing toward the rear of the horse. A well-trained horse won't mind your starting with his left or right leg, but it is wise to start with his left if he's inexperienced or nervous because he's more used to being approached on his left. Run your hand down the horse's leg, and if he does not automatically pick it up for you, squeeze gently at the indentation between bone and tendon just above the fetlock joint. This

> ## AT A GLANCE
>
> Daily handling and cleaning of feet will tell you:
>
> • When feet need to be trimmed or reshod.
>
> • When feet are cracked, chipped, or bruised.
>
> • When there is heat in the feet or legs or swelling in the lower leg.

pressure will encourage him to pick it up. Tickling or pressing gently at the heel will also stimulate a young foal to pick up the foot. Pinch the chestnut (horny growth on the inside of the upper front leg) on a horse that does not want to lift the foot. This produces a reflex that lifts the foot. Because the leg is lifted automatically and immediately, don't be in the way or his knee may smash your nose. For cleaning or trimming, hold the foot between your legs.

To pick up a hind foot, again make sure the horse can balance on the other three legs. Stand close to the horse and run your hand down the leg, squeezing gently at the fetlock joint if he doesn't pick the foot up readily. Lean against a reluctant horse to encourage him to shift his weight to the other legs and pick up this one. For cleaning and trimming, rest the leg across your thigh.

Training a Young Horse for Trimming and Shoeing

If you start handling feet regularly when the horse is a foal, he will be well mannered by the time he needs trimming. His first trim may be at a few weeks to a few months of age, depending on wear and conformation — whether he needs a bit of correction early on. If a foal is nervous, hold onto the foot (rather than the leg) after picking it up, and don't hold it off the ground very high. Until he gets used to the handling, this method is less threatening than holding onto the leg or holding the foot high. It's also less traumatic if the foal is standing next to a wall or next to his mother so he has the support and security of something solid on the other side. Start with a hind foot because it's easier for him to balance with a hind off the ground than with a front. Do one side first; then, the other.

After getting a foal accustomed to shifting his weight and letting you pick up a foot, don't just pick up each foot for a few seconds and put it right back down again. Hold a foot in shoeing position (between your legs for a front foot, across your thigh for a hind) and actually clean it. If he gets accustomed to holding the hoof up for a longer period, he will be less impatient when the time comes for trimming and then shoeing. Tap on the hoof wall with your hoof pick to get him used to the feel of the tapping.

Young horses, like young children, have short attention spans and not much patience. When you start actual trimming, keep the youngster happy and comfortable. Hold the foot in a position that will not cause anxiety or discomfort — not too high (especially a hind foot) or out to the side. Legs only bend within a specific range, limited by certain joints. Don't put any strain on them or flex the leg very much.

This is also crucial when trimming or shoeing an older horse that might have arthritic, painful joints or a sore back; or a horse with an old injury that might be stressed if you keep the leg flexed too long. In these situations keep the foot as low as you can while working on it. Don't hold the leg at such an angle that it might cause pain or pull it out from the body at shoulder or hip. Your position should be dictated by the horse's comfort. A tall, lean, muscled horse can usually hold his feet up higher and longer without discomfort than a shorter or heavily muscled horse.

Sometimes a horse with arthritis or some other type of leg

or joint discomfort becomes uncomfortable if you hold a leg too long because of the extra weight on the supporting leg. The horse may try to take his foot away (or may even try to lie down) because he needs both feet on the ground to support himself comfortably.

Work smoothly and swiftly; put the leg down again before the horse becomes impatient and wants to take it away from you. This may mean doing part of the job, putting the foot down, going on to the next, and coming back to the first foot after the horse has had a chance to stand on it for a while. For a young or nervous horse, you can clean each foot, make the rounds again with the hoof nippers, then come back to each foot again for final rasping and smoothing. That way the youngster doesn't have to hold one foot up for what seems to him an unbearable length of time while you do the whole job. Alternating work on each leg in short stints gives the horse a positional rest and he is more comfortable. The same principle applies when shoeing an inexperienced or nervous horse — he may tolerate your working on a foot for a short time only.

If you are slow and methodical while learning to shoe, do your first shoeings on patient horses. Let your farrier continue to do young ones or restless ones until you've become more proficient and can do them more quickly. This saves a lot of frustration for both you and the horse; you always want the trimming and shoeing to be well tolerated by the horse and not turned into a wrestling match.

CLEANING THE FEET

A hoof pick is the best tool for cleaning the foot though you can also use the blunt edge of a hoof knife to get the dirt out. Never use a sharp or pointed instrument for cleaning a hoof; you might injure yourself or the horse if he jerks his foot. Always use something blunt when cleaning dirt or muck away from the cleft between frog and sole. Anything sharp could injure the sensitive tissues beneath the cleft —

Using a hoof pick.

especially toward the heel where soft tissues are closer to the surface. If you clean the clefts from heel to toe, you are less likely to poke too hard into the heel area than if you clean a cleft from toe to heel.

Any dead tissue along the sole can be removed with a hoof knife. When you are trimming the foot, you may need to attend to the frog if it is overgrown. If the foot is healthy, the frog probably needs no trimming other than just smoothing up and getting rid of loose tags and tatters.

Most horses shed the frog twice a year. Sometimes the old part is still hanging there (or pieces of it) or sticking out at the back of the foot (still attached at the back). If this happens, the old part should be carefully trimmed away with the hoof knife or hoof nippers. Otherwise, the shedding portion may become dry and stiff, sometimes curling up and poking the skin above the back of the heel. As the frog is shed, new healthy tissue grows in underneath to replace it, but this takes some time. For a while some hooves may look almost frogless until the new frog grows in.

A thrushy frog — which is common if the horse lives in damp or muddy conditions — may need to be trimmed more than a healthy frog to get rid of pockets of infection and get down to healthy frog tissue. If the frog is undermined and rotten with thrush, all abnormal portions should be trimmed so the area can be treated to eliminate the thrush infection.

TRIMMING

Assessing the Foot

Some horse owners leave trimming and shoeing to a farrier while others do the trimming themselves — especially if they have several horses that don't need to be shod, such as broodmares or lightly used pleasure horses.

The first step in trimming a horse is careful observation of feet and leg position when he is standing squarely. This gives an idea of his normal hoof/pastern angles and whether they are proper for his construction or out of kilter due to excessive hoof growth. He should be able to stand squarely (with feet directly under his shoulders and hips), with each foot properly supporting his body weight. If he is not comfortable standing squarely at rest and usually stands with one leg pointing forward or outward, this indicates discomfort or imbalance. Have a veterinarian or a professional farrier check him.

Then observe him in motion at both the walk and trot to see how he handles his feet — whether they move relatively straight, paddle outward, or wing inward. If you have observed your horse in motion or followed behind while someone else is riding him, you should already be familiar with how your horse travels; however, it's always good to observe him again just before you trim his feet. Notice the point at which the foot breaks over and leaves the ground — whether the breakover point is at the center of the toe where it should be or off to one side. Also, note any abnormal deviation in foot flight.

Look at the bottom of the horse's feet or at his old shoes before you start to trim the feet or remove the shoes for trimming. Uneven wear of the feet (one side of the hoof wall longer than the other or one side of the toe worn off) shows the horse is not traveling straight but is breaking over to one side and also landing out of balance. A horse that travels straight on sound feet and legs will wear his feet (or shoes) evenly, with slightly more wear at the center of the toe.

An off-center wear spot to the outside of the toe means the horse is probably toeing in. If the wear spot is on the inside of the toe, the horse is toeing out. Proper trimming and balancing of the foot can correct this somewhat, but overzealous "correction" of crooked legs can make a horse lame if it puts unnatural stresses on joints and supportive structures (see Chapter 8). Unless the horse is interfering (hitting one limb against the other), don't worry about it.

Determine the proper foot angle for the horse, and try to trim the foot to accommodate that angle. Hind legs generally have more upright feet and pasterns than front legs. Not every horse has the same hoof angles, and some horses may have a different angle for each foot and should be trimmed accordingly (see Chapter 2). Trying to make the feet match on a horse with one club foot, for instance, may make him severely lame. Each horse's feet must be trimmed and balanced to fit his individual conformation.

Each foot should be trimmed so pastern and hoof form an unbroken angle line, whatever the angle is for that foot. If toes are left too long, the angle line is broken, straining tendons and joints. If the heel is too long, the line will be broken the other direction. With the horse standing squarely, study the foot to judge how much hoof wall must be trimmed to level the foot at its proper angle.

Looking at a horse's shoulder angle can often help determine what his foot angle should be because angles in a horse's body tend to be similar. A relatively steep (upright) shoulder usually corresponds with an upright foot, while a more sloping shoulder corresponds with a more sloping foot. Hind feet may be a little steeper than the front, but when the feet are trimmed in balance, they often are nearly the same.

Also, keep in mind that when viewed from the side, heels should have the same slope as the front of the hoof. The hoof wall at the toe has the same angle with the ground as the hoof wall at the heel. If heels are more upright than the toe, the horse has a club foot. If the heels are more sloped than the toe, they are underrun. Either condition needs special attention when being trimmed.

The base of support, when the horse is standing squarely, should extend back to a line that descends from the center of the cannon bone to the ground. The back of his heel should be at that point, below the center of the cannon. If the heel doesn't extend quite that far back, the heels of the shoe generally need to — if the horse is shod — for best support and to encourage the foot to grow properly to regain that support.

The foot should also be balanced from side to side as well as front to back, allowing for the slight difference in outside and inside slant of the hoof wall. Lack of balance in the hoof causes uneven stress distribution. This can lead to strain on the leg, problems with hoof wear and gait, and possible interference.

> ## AT A GLANCE
>
> Before you trim:
>
> • Observe foot angles while the horse is standing squarely.
>
> • Observe feet in motion.
>
> • Check bottom of foot or old shoe for wear patterns.

You can assess side-to-side foot balance (but not front/back foot balance) by watching the horse move to see if one side of the foot lands before the other. You can also "look down the leg" when you pick up a foot, holding the cannon bone just below the knee (or hock), to let the foot hang loosely. This gives a view of the ground surface of the foot and whether it is hanging in balance, perpendicular to an imaginary line continued down from the center of the cannon bone — with the inside and outside heels level. A just-removed worn horseshoe can provide an even more accurate assessment.

When you trim the foot, make the ground surface of the hoof wall as level as possible. (Trimming in preparation for applying a shoe will be covered in the next chapter.) If the horse is to go barefoot, leave about a 1/4-inch of hoof wall projecting below the sole, especially if he has been wearing shoes and is not accustomed to being barefoot. Don't take quite as much hoof off as you would for shoeing or the horse may become tenderfooted quickly while walking on his sole. The area between the hoof wall and sole has not had a

Using the nippers.

Rasping the edges.

chance to toughen up yet.

The barefoot horse needs a little extra horn tissue to keep sharp rocks and gravel from breaking into sensitive structures. The outside edge of the entire foot should be smoothed and rounded with the rasp to keep it from splitting or chipping. Rounding the edges also helps prevent injury to other horses if several horses are running together. Kick wounds or cuts on the lower legs often result from a foot being stepped on or a leg hitting the sharp snags of other horses' untrimmed hooves.

Trimming Intervals

How often a horse needs trimming depends on many factors, particularly how fast his hooves grow. A shod horse usually needs trimming every four to 10 weeks (depending on his growth rate) because there is no way for the hoof to wear naturally. (Feet tend to grow faster in summer and slower in winter, but there will be a more consistent difference between individuals than between seasons.)

If the horse is barefoot, trimming intervals may depend almost entirely on how fast his feet wear. If he has ideal conditions for space and exercise, he should wear the hooves at about the same rate they grow; they seldom need trimming. The feet may occasionally need to be smoothed to prevent or halt chipping or cracking, but very little hoof wall needs to be removed.

By contrast, a horse in a stall, pen, or soft pasture will need regular foot trimming. If the foot does not have ideal conditions, it may need trimming even more often than if the horse were wearing shoes — to keep the foot from splitting or cracking in dry conditions or splaying out in wet conditions. In poor environments, shoes can protect the foot that would otherwise break or crack. Diligent and frequent trimming and smoothing may be necessary.

Similarly, a horse with a foot problem (severe crack, chronic founder) needs to be trimmed often. With an unbalanced foot or a chronic problem in which part of the horn grows faster, frequent trimming to remove the regrown horn can keep the foot at its most ideal shape and balance. Trimming can also relieve pressure on a crack and help it grow out faster. A severely cracked foot may continue to crack if a hoof is allowed to grow much between trimming intervals; the long foot puts more widening forces on the crack.

There are no specific guidelines for how often a horse's hooves need to be trimmed. You must figure this out for yourself, taking each horse's individual needs into consideration. The worst thing about this lack of specific guidelines is that some horse owners leave the shoes on too long — sometimes so long that the shoes eventually come loose and fall off on their own — and the feet don't get trimmed as often as they should.

A horse whose feet have grown too long because shoes are left on may suffer leg wounds, striking himself with long hooves. He may also be at risk for strained legs, contracted feet, corns, and other injuries due to long feet and shoe pressure. Because the hoof wall grows perpendicularly from the coronary band, the horse's base of support grows out from under him if shoes are left on too long. This strains flexor tendons and the navicular bone inside the hoof, as well as all foot and leg joints. Shoes worn too long may become thin and loose, sometimes bending and shifting, causing corns (from pressure on bars or sole) or nail punctures. The healthiest situation is to trim and shoe at more appropriate intervals.

CHAPTER 4
Basic Shoeing

Shoeing is neither complicated nor difficult if you have the desire and strength to do it and if your horses cooperate — which they should if you have handled their feet regularly. It's handy to be able to take care of your horse's feet because you won't have to wait for a busy farrier who might not be able to work you into his schedule for a few days.

Even if you never do any shoeing yourself, it's always good to learn all you can about your horses' feet and to know how shoeing should be done. This chapter is not meant to be a substitute for shoeing school or lessons from a professional farrier. Its purpose is to help you understand more about shoeing and to give some tips and explanations if you are thinking about learning to do your own.

Your own horses are perfect to learn on. Because you've handled their feet in all seasons, all circumstances, you know how their feet grow and have seen them in action thousands of times. If you have been observant, you know how your horses travel and how their feet wear, and you should know how your horses' feet should be trimmed and shod to have proper foot balance and to travel best with least hindrance from shoes. Your own horses know you, trust you, and are accustomed to how you handle their feet.

ASSESSING OLD SHOES

If a horse has been previously shod, carefully assess the old shoes before and after you remove them. They can reveal a lot about the horse's feet and the previous shoeing job. Looking at the shoes before they are removed, you can tell if they weren't wide enough at the heels for adequate hoof expansion. The hoof wall at the heels and quarters may be starting to grow down around the shoe. This, however, can sometimes happen even in a well-fitted shoe left on too long.

> ## AT A GLANCE
>
> • Learn all you can about your horses' feet, whether you shoe them yourself or not.
>
> • Old shoes provide details about a horse's feet and how it travels.
>
> • Trim from heel to toe or in a complete circle.
>
> • Fit the shoe to the foot, not the foot to the shoe.

When you look at a properly fitted shoe after removal, it usually has some grooves at the heel (on the side that was next to the hoof) where constant expansion and contraction of the hoof have worn a little of the shoe away. If the hoof side of a used shoe is as smooth as new in the heel areas, the heel of the hoof may have been "nailbound" (too tightly nailed) to the shoe, could not expand and contract, and was pinched every time the horse put weight on that foot.

The old shoe can provide clues on how to trim the foot and fit the new shoe, whether to use a different type of shoe, etc. You can tell whether the shoe was strong and hard enough to last, whether it wore out too fast, or whether to modify the next trimming and shoeing to help the horse travel straighter.

One part of the shoe being worn

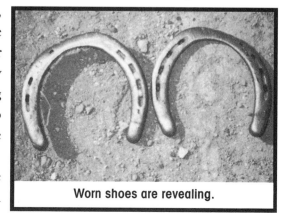

Worn shoes are revealing.

more than another indicates unequal stress. Thin or worn spots in the old shoe indicate which side of the hoof is more loaded. Some type of imbalance caused the horse to put more weight on a specific area of the foot, such as landing on the inside branch or outside branch instead of squarely or breaking over the side of the toe instead of the center. An off-center wear spot means the foot toes in or out (not facing straight forward) and is not being picked up straight. Getting the front/back balance (see Chapter 2) correct and making sure the foot lands relatively equally on both sides will take care of the problem.

Compare right and left shoes (front and hind feet) and also the front and back shoes on the same side. Differences in shoe wear between right and left indicate unequal use, either from an uneven gait or from a one-sided rider. Uneven wear may indicate different foot angles (such as one club foot), or it may be the first indication of unsoundness because a subtle lameness can make a horse use the lame and sound legs differently.

A crooked saddle tree, a rider who sits crookedly (with more weight in one stirrup or one stirrup shorter than the other), or a rider who always posts on the same diagonal at the trot may cause a horse to use his legs unevenly — adjusting his body and stride to compensate for the rider's imbalance. A sound horse travels symmetrically (if properly trimmed and shod) and should wear his feet or shoes evenly, unless improper riding or equipment hinders his gait.

TRIMMING IN PREPARATION FOR THE SHOE

After thoroughly cleaning the foot with a hoof pick, trim dead tissue (any flaking off portions or loose tags) from the sole or frog with a hoof knife. Any loose material can be scraped away, but don't trim any deeper unless the horse has an abnormal buildup of dead material. He needs this horny sole as protection from bruising. Most horses don't need any paring away of the sole, except maybe a little dead tissue around the outer edges next to the hoof wall — to give an indication of where to make the cuts with the hoof nippers. This will help you place the nippers correctly to cut the wall down to the level of the sole.

Trim the outer hoof wall with hoof nippers, keeping the hoof wall level with the sole except at the quarters. Hoof nippers should be held so they make a flat, level cut and, thus, a level seat for the shoe. When you are trimming the hoof wall, you must usually leave a little at the quarters to achieve a flat surface because the sole is concave there — not the same level as at heel or toe. Remember the four-point trim; the quarters break away in a bare foot. When you are putting a shoe on a horse, however, you want the hoof's surface to be smooth, with no gaps. If you cut the quarters level with the sole, you'll have cut away too much and the wall will not meet the shoe at this spot. The only time you want a gap (where the hoof wall does not meet the shoe) is to relieve pressure on a hoof crack — so it won't continue to split due to weight-bearing forces.

Trimming can be done from heel to toe on both sides or in a complete circle from heel to heel for a smooth and consistent cut. Or you can start at the toe and work to each heel. Carefully judge how much hoof wall to leave at the heel for a level foot and proper hoof angle. Trim the hoof wall level with the sole at the toe and as low or high as needed at the heel to keep the horse's normal foot angle. The toe should be trimmed completely; remember the natural foot of the free-roaming horse, where the toe is worn completely away.

If bars need trimming, trim them level with the hoof wall at the heels, but no more. The horse needs bars for support. After excess hoof wall has been trimmed away, rasp the area smooth to make a level seat for the shoe. The shoe must rest smoothly on the foot without any "rocking." If a shoe does not meet the foot perfectly flat, there will be some movement that wears on the nails (which may wear through, causing the shoe to come off) and may split the hoof.

The rasp should always be held flat and level so one side of the hoof is not accidentally made lower than the other. This is important because leveling the foot can be difficult when the horse's body inhibits the swing of your arm. Some right-handed farriers have trouble leveling a horse's right front foot. Some left-handed farriers have trouble leveling the left front; with the horse's belly in the way, movement of that hand and arm is hindered.

Right-handed farriers tend to leave the outside of the toe and inside of the heel on the right front foot a little long. The foot becomes unbalanced over time, concentrating the weight and loading in these areas. Lameness can result. This condition is so common it is nicknamed right front foot disease or right-handed shoer's disease. It must be corrected with careful trimming, gradually adjusting hoof length to balance the foot again and to restore uniform weight bearing and wear.

After you have trimmed and rasped the foot smooth, remeasure the hoof angle and double check the levelness of the hoof wall. The shoe should contact the hoof wall completely and cover up the white line, but should barely touch the sole — covering about 1/8- to 1/4-inch of the sole. If too much of the shoe rests on the sole, the pressure may cause bruising and lameness. With a normal foot, this is rarely a problem, even with a wide-webbed shoe, because the sole has some concavity, drawing away from the shoe. With a flat-footed horse, however, the shoe may need to be concave on

Smooth the edges with a rasp.

the edge next to the sole to avoid excessive sole pressure.

Once the foot is trimmed and level, shape the shoe to fit the foot. The farrier's rule is to fit the shoe to the foot, not the foot to the shoe. This prevents sloppy shoeing in which a shoe is poorly fitted and then whatever portion of hoof wall extends beyond the shoe is rasped off. But this rule certainly does not mean the shoe should accommodate the distorted shape of an unbalanced foot.

Flares, distortions of hoof wall caused by an uneven weight load, should be removed or minimized before the shoe is fitted. A flare (or spreading forward) at the toe creates a dished effect and makes the toe too long for proper balance and breakover. A flare at one side makes the foot unbalanced from side to side; it puts stress on the leg and alters the gait. Flared areas should be rasped to more normal shape to ensure proper weight bearing and to encourage normal hoof growth and shape. If left uncorrected, a flare usually gets worse, adding more stress to the leg. It may lead to hoof cracking because the wall is so distorted; the uneven stress can create breaking and tearing.

FITTING A SHOE

Factory-made shoes can be easily fitted to most horses, once the foot has been balanced, just by spreading the shoes at the heels as much as needed and changing the shoes' shape slightly on the anvil. For most horses, if you've chosen the proper size, a shoe merely needs to be spread or spread and then rounded to fit the contour at the heels more perfectly.

Factory shoes may stick out a little too much in front. If you don't have a forge for heating the metal to roll the toe, it can be squared off across the front with a cutting torch. For a well-balanced foot, the toe needs to be short, like the natural bare foot. A short, squared toe also helps the horse break over center rather than off to one side. If you are not a welder or a blacksmith, and the shoes need to be altered more than you can do on an anvil, have an experienced person help you.

The shoe should be slightly wider than the hoof (about 1/16 of an inch) at the quarters and heels to allow for expansion when weight is placed on it. The shoe should extend just beyond the heels of the foot so the heels always have the support of the shoe. Then they won't be vulnerable to stone bruising and also won't grow down around the back of the shoe (creating abnormal pressure on the bars and heel tissues) if the shoes are left on too long. The shoe must allow for a little extra width to accommodate quarters and heels, which expand every time they take weight. When you look at the foot from above (when the horse is standing on it), you should just barely see the edge of the shoe, from the quarters to the heels.

If the shoe is too short or does not fit properly at heels and quarters, the shoe may press into the foot as the hoof wall grows, creating a corn (See Chapter 7). If the shoe is too narrow or short, the hoof tends to expand over the shoe when weight is placed on it, or the narrow shoe limits proper hoof expansion.

Because the foot must be allowed to expand when bearing weight, especially at the heels, nails should never be driven into the hoof too far back. The last nail hole of the shoe should not be farther back than the bend of the quarter. A nail beyond this point limits hoof expansion.

The shoe should be properly centered on the foot. For horses with good leg conformation and normal feet (straight and balanced), the shoe can be centered by using the point of the frog as a guide. The frog will divide the bottom of the foot equally and point toward

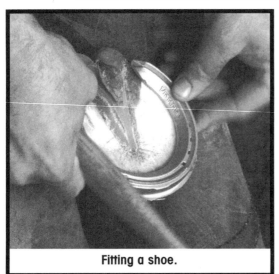

Fitting a shoe.

the center of the toe. In pigeon-toed or splay-footed horses, however, the frog usually points off center and cannot be used as a guide.

If a hoof is worn excessively on one side because of poor conformation or faulty gait (or if part of the hoof wall has chipped and broken away), it might not be possible to make the foot perfectly level by trimming; you'd have to trim too much away on the opposite side. If one side of the foot is broken or very low, the branch of the shoe on that side can be shimmed with leather so the shod foot will be level. When the hoof wall has grown out by the next shoeing, the foot can be trimmed normally, with no need to shim the shoe.

> ## AT A GLANCE
>
> • The shoe should fit evenly on the foot.
>
> • The bottom of the hoof wall should rest flat against the shoe.
>
> • The heels of the shoe should not extend much behind the foot (1/16- to 1/8- of an inch), especially on the front feet.
>
> • The outer edge of the shoe should closely follow the outline of the trimmed hoof at the toe.

DRIVING THE NAILS

When the shoe has been properly shaped to fit the trimmed and balanced foot, the nails can be driven. Use properly sized nails for the hoof and shoe. Make sure the nail head protrudes a little from the crease of the shoe after being driven in. A nail head that fits too deeply into the crease is too small and won't hold as well; the shoe may work loose. Nails too large, with heads too big to sink into the shoe crease, will also create problems. The nail head will quickly wear away, leaving nothing to secure the shoe.

The nails should enter the hoof at the white line area, curving out through the hoof wall when driven. When nailing the shoe on, hold the nail with thumb and index finger, resting your hand on the shoe to keep it stable and in proper position as you drive the first nail.

The location of the first nail does not matter much. You can start with the right or left side, near the toe or heel. The main thing is to keep the shoe properly centered and in place during driving of the nail. Keep in mind that if a shoe is going to shift while you drive that first nail, it tends to work back from the toe. Knowing this, you can compensate a bit and have it end exactly where you want it. After the first two nails are driven — one on each side of the shoe — the shoe will stay in place as you drive in the rest. It will also stay in place if you have to set the foot down momentarily before putting in the other nails (as when shoeing a nervous young horse for the first time), or you want to check how well the shoe fits with the horse standing on it.

Horseshoe nails are made with a straight side and a beveled side so they will curve when driven. The beveled side of the nail point should always be toward the inside of the foot so the nail will be directed outward as it is driven. With some brands of horseshoe nails, the beveled side can be easily determined by the rough side of the nail head; the bevel and the rough side are both on the inside. Using the rough edge as a guide, you can tell which way to set the nail just by the feel of the nail head.

The nail should be aimed for the spot where it should come out of the hoof wall (to take a short, thick hold). If driven too straight in, nails may come out too high, especially on a horse with small feet. In most instances, you want the nail to come out about 3/4-inch above the shoe, or no more than a third of the way up the hoof wall. The actual distance will depend, of course, on the size of the horse and its feet, as well as nail length. A draft horse, for instance, will need larger shoes and nails than a pony or an Arabian, and the nails can come up a little higher in the hoof wall because there is so much more wall above them. If a nail comes out much too high or too low, however, it should be pulled and driven again. If the nail is bent or curved after you pull it out, use a new nail.

If you see a nail is not going to come out at the desired spot and will be too high, pull it out before you drive it all the way in. It will be much easier to pull at that point. Also, a high nail may press on the sensitive tissues inside the foot and make the horse lame. You don't want to drive it all the way in.

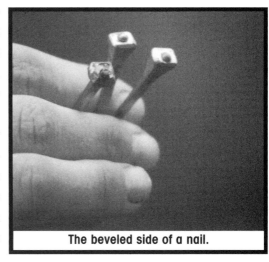

The beveled side of a nail.

A low nail may break out the side of the hoof and be of no use in holding the shoe. Nails driven to a uniform height give the shod hoof a pleasing appearance, but if they come out anywhere near the proper position it's best to leave them. A nail pulled and driven again just to make a uniform appearance may weaken the wall.

The nails should be driven in the same direction as the hoof fibers, parallel to them, to minimize cutting them and weakening the hoof wall. Hoof fibers grow parallel to each other and perpendicular to the coronary band at the top of the hoof. The driven nails should go into the outer portion of the hoof wall, never inside the white line that separates the wall from the sole — or they'll go into the sensitive part of the foot.

The white line is an important landmark during shoeing, as the hoof wall and sole unite there. Driven nails can enter at or near the white line but should always stay outside it on their journey through the hoof wall — curving outward. They should be placed correctly (beveled tip to the inside) so they will curve and come out the side of the hoof wall rather than curving into the sensitive part of the foot.

A high nail is more apt to prick sensitive tissues than a low one or put pressure on those tissues if it bends a bit inside the hoof wall. If a horse flinches during the driving of a nail, the sensitive tissues may have been pricked or nicked. If this happens, the nail should be pulled out and iodine squirted into the nail hole to prevent infection — especially if blood appears on the nail or in the hole where you pulled it out.

If you use light hammer taps when driving the nail, the point of the nail will travel parallel to the horn fibers and won't sever them. To drive the nail through the side of the outer wall at the desired place, use light hammer taps until the nail is about two-thirds of the required distance, and then strike one hard blow to force the nail through the wall to finish its journey. The bevel on the nail point makes the nail curve outward, and this bevel is most effective in curving the nail when it's being driven sharply and rapidly (traveling faster) through the horn fibers.

As soon as a nail is driven through and the nail head is sunk into the shoe crease, twist the sharp tip end off with the hammer claws or cut the end off with nail cutters. Keep track of the nail tips so you can discard them properly. Do not leave them lying on the ground to cause a flat tire. The sharp nail tips should always be taken off as soon as each nail is driven, so that if the horse moves or tries to take his foot away from you, the sharp end won't cut your leg. Always wear a leather shoeing apron or thick leather chaps to protect your legs when driving nails.

CLINCHING THE NAILS

After all the nails have been driven and the tips cut or twisted off, see if any of the protruding ends are too long. You may need to cut some of them off closer to the hoof wall so they won't create an excessively long clinch. Then cut a small notch underneath each clipped nail with a rasp. This notch will keep the hoof wall from splitting when the nail end is turned over and clinched. It will also remove the piece of hoof horn directly beneath the clinch — which otherwise tends to roll down with the nail tip as you clinch it, making a lump under the nail and preventing a good, tight clinch.

The notch also provides a place for the clinch. The nail end, when clinched, will be sunk into this little space and make a smooth surface on the hoof wall. A clinch well sunk into the hoof

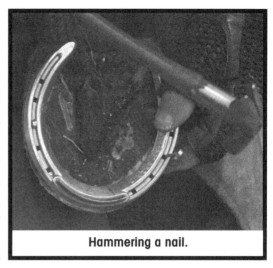

Hammering a nail.

wall won't get knocked loose as readily when the horse is traveling through rocks, and if it's tight and smooth against the hoof wall, it won't nick the opposite leg as the horse travels.

To clinch the nails, pound each nail head tightly into the shoe crease while holding a piece of iron (with a good square edge) against the tip, to bend the tip over into the notch you cut, as the nail is driven farther out of the hoof wall. The edge of a rasp will work for this if you have nothing else at hand.

Nails should be clinched alternately from one side to the other, starting first with the two toe nails, or the two heel nails, rather than clinching all the nails on one side and then on the other. Clinching them alternately from side to side gives a tighter, more uniform seating of the shoe. Nails should be clinched firmly, but not so

Clipping the nail ends.

tightly that they make the horse's foot sore and "nail bound." If you clinch the nails too tightly, the horse may be tender for a few days.

Finish the clinch by bending the nails down firmly with a hammer (pounding the tips flat down against the hoof wall, into the notch) or by using a clinching tool. The latter is like a pair of pliers with a curved gripping edge that fits the angle of the hoof wall. This tool puts a squeeze on the turned-over nail and pushes it down flat and into the little groove you cut next to the nail. The clinches will be flush with the hoof wall and feel smooth when you run your hand over them.

A short, tight clinch holds better and is neater than a long one; a long clinch doesn't fit into the notch and protrudes a little from the hoof wall — with more chance of being knocked and unbent in the rocks. It could thus work loose more easily, unless it's very tight. A clinch too short, however, may not hold because it can pull back through the nail hole; if the shoe catches on anything, it can be very easily pulled off. Clinches should usually be about as long as the nail is wide — with a square appearance.

How short the clinches should be depends upon the horse's job. Many farriers prefer very short, neat clinches. These do not detract from the hoof's appearance (for a show horse) and also open up easily and allow the nails to pull back through the hoof if the shoe catches on something — letting the shoe come off cleanly without tearing chunks out of the hoof wall. But to avoid losing a shoe before it's time for reshoeing, some horsemen prefer slightly longer and more durable clinches.

Nails should take a short, thick hold on the hoof wall and not be too high. A nail going through the hoof wall at an angle, coming out 3/4-inch above the shoe, has a lot more holding power than a high nail (coming out an inch or more above the shoe); the high nail is relatively straight and requires less force to pull it back out. A nail with a short, thick hold damages the least amount of hoof horn — it has gone a shorter distance through the wall — and the old nail holes can be removed with the growth of the hoof the next time the horse is shod. This is important if the horse is being used steadily (endurance riding, checking cattle daily on a rocky range, traveling on pavement or gravel roads, etc.) and wears out his shoes at a fast rate. If the horse must be shod often, you want room in the hoof wall for the new nails for each new set of shoes.

When you finish clinching the nails, use a rasp to smooth the outside edge where hoof meets shoe. Most shoeing books caution the shoer to be careful not to rasp the outside of the hoof wall too much. Some say rasping removes the periople. In actuality the periople (similar to the cuticle on a human fingernail) rarely extends more than an inch below the hairline at the coronary band and is easy to see when the hoof is wet.

The horny wall is made up of tiny tubes (the horn fibers), protected on the outside surface by the very thin stratum tectorium that extends down the length of the hoof. Excessive rasping can remove this and cut the horn tubules — leaving them open and allowing the hoof to dry out. But this is not so critical that it justifies ignoring an unbalanced hoof that needs to have a flare on one side trimmed off or the toe trimmed back to proper position.

On a balanced foot, if the shoe has been properly fitted to the hoof to begin with and nailed on with no slipping, little or no rasping will be needed on the outside of the hoof wall to smooth it to the shoe. The only exception might be some rasping at the toe to keep it short and at the proper breakover point. On a foot that needs more rasping for balance, a good hoof sealant can replace the protection that's been lost.

After the horse is shod, have someone lead him at both the walk and the trot (straight away and straight back to you, and also at a trot directly past you) so you can observe the new shoes and the horse's feet in action. Then you can determine if the shoes are set properly and not hindering his gait; you can also make sure the horse is not lame or "ouchy" from the new shoes.

DEALING WITH A QUICKED NAIL

Occasionally a horse is a little tender after being newly shod. Usually this is just a temporary soreness if the clinches are a little too tight. But if the horse is sore on only one foot and the soreness becomes more acute during the next twenty-four to forty-eight hours, this is cause for concern.

Sometimes a horse with a nail too close to inner tissues of the foot (slightly inside the white line) is not lame immediately but may become lame a few days after shoeing. The nail may have been driven too high or has shifted a little, creating pressure and pain. Hoof testers can reveal the offending nail so it can be removed. To help narrow the possibilities as to which nail it might be, lead the horse in circles to determine whether the foot is sorer on the inside or the outside branch of the shoe. If there is any chance the nail has pricked sensitive tissues, make sure the horse's tetanus protection is up to date.

The shoe does not necessarily have to be removed to find the problem nail. Tapping each nail with a hammer may reveal the culprit; the horse will flinch and try to take his foot away when the bad nail is tapped. Then you can unclinch and remove it, pulling it out by grasping the nail head with hoof pincers.

Usually once the offending nail is removed and the puncture (nail hole) disinfected, the problem resolves rapidly. The horse should get over the lameness in a day or two. If the nail hole has become infected, however, it may be necessary to treat the horse with antibiotics and soak the foot (as you would for a puncture wound) until the infection and lameness are gone.

In some cases the shoe must be removed to aid in diagnosis or treatment of the puncture, but if the problem is discovered soon, removing the nail and disinfecting the hole with iodine may be all that's needed. The horse can be back in use in a day or two. If the shoe was securely nailed on, it will hold until the next shoeing, even with one nail missing. If the nail is in a location that really needs a nail, another one can be put in, aimed in a slightly different direction to make sure it enters the outer hoof wall and not the sensitive tissues.

CHAPTER 5

Types of Shoes

There are many kinds of horseshoes; try to select shoes well suited to your horse's work. While a horse with a problem may need a farrier to create a special shoe, many horses get along fine with factory-made shoes.

Shoes should always be as light as is practical, taking into consideration the wear demanded of them, so that they interfere as little as possible with the normal flight of the horse's foot. Weight, no matter how it's added to the foot, tends to reduce speed and agility. Added weight can also make a minor deviation in foot flight more noticeable.

The normal flight of the foot is a relatively straightforward line. No horse's foot moves perfectly straight, but good leg conformation creates the most straightforward motion with the least wasted effort and movement. Any significant deviation from normal foot flight takes the form of an arc — either to the outside or inside of this relatively straight line. Adding weight to the foot in the form of a shoe will increase the arc because of the additional swing it makes. Ordinary shoeing thus accentuates a horse's foot flight and any gait defect.

Most horses never hit themselves when running barefoot (with short, properly worn hooves) but some will forge or interfere when shod, due to the added weight of the shoe. A horse that tends to interfere (strike one front limb against the other, or one hind limb against the other hind) or forge (strike a front heel or sole with the hind toe) does so even worse when shod. The weight makes the horse's strides slightly longer and the arcs of foot flight even more pronounced. Thus, he must be carefully (correctively) shod to prevent these problems.

A horse that toes in usually breaks over to the outside and swings his foot outward (paddling), whereas a horse that toes out tends to break over the inside and swing the foot inward (winging). Therefore, the toed-out horse is more apt to interfere while a toed-in horse almost never does. A horse's conformation may also play a part in forging. A short-backed horse with long legs is more apt to forge than a horse with legs proportionate to his body length. However, these are generalizations; some individuals don't fit the pattern due to other aspects of their conformation.

If you have a horse that hits himself and the problem is not corrected enough by squaring the toe to help him break over straight, he may need special shoeing. You may need a lighter shoe or help from a professional farrier. Before you attempt to shoe the horse yourself, seek advice from your farrier on how to shoe the horse to minimize the problem, or just let the professional do it. Always keep in mind that too much "correction" can cause lameness (see Chapter 8).

STEEL SHOES

Steel shoes are commonly used for ordinary shoeing. Compared to most other material, steel is relatively inexpensive, easy to work with, and very durable. Unless a horse is used very hard, a steel shoe will generally last until the next shoeing. The disadvantages of steel are its heaviness and poor ability to dissipate concussion. In some disciplines, such as racing, lighter shoes are preferable.

ALUMINUM SHOES

Aluminum shoes are lighter than steel ones but cost more

and wear out more quickly. Cast aluminum is about one-third the weight of steel but not as durable — and harder to weld and work with. Extruded aluminum is less brittle and can be shaped hot or cold. Being lighter, aluminum shoes are also more flexible, a factor that can contribute to hoof wall stress in some instances. Aluminum's flexibility, however, can vary greatly, depending on how it's combined with other metals. Some aluminum shoes are stiffer than some types of steel shoes. Aluminum shoes can be made wider and thinner than steel shoes, giving the horse more base of support if needed, with less weight.

TITANIUM SHOES

Titanium shoes are as light as aluminum shoes but more durable and more expensive.

GLUE-ON SHOES

Plastic, rubber, and other types of glue-on shoes have come into use in recent years but are most commonly used for foals or horses with hoof disease or hoof injuries — situations in which it's better not to put nails into the hoof wall. One disadvantage of using most types of glue-on shoes is there's no give in the heel area. A shoe glued all around the hoof wall

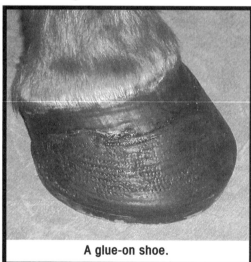

A glue-on shoe.

inhibits expansion of the heels. Also, plastic and glue-on shoes generally do not hold up well enough for horses doing hard work.

Many innovations and improvements have been made in glue-on shoes. There are new types of glue-on shoes with a cuff that goes over the hoof wall; the shoe is glued to the bottom of the foot and also to the wall, thus staying on better. Another type of glue-on shoe incorporates a layer that reduces impact concussion. Some farriers have developed ways to glue aluminum racing plates to the foot, enabling horses with poor feet that won't hold nails to continue racing.

TRACTION

A horse's ability to work with optimum agility and balance depends a lot upon his shoes. The foot needs a certain amount of traction to grip the ground and keep from sliding around too much, yet it must be able to slide a little — or the abrupt stop and jar could cause serious injury. The horse needs the right amount of traction and "give" each time the foot comes to the ground and pushes off again.

Because shoeing a barefoot horse can change or eliminate traction, choose or adapt shoes to suit a particular horse's traction needs. The best ground-side surface of a shoe, for most horses, is plain, without heel and toe reinforcements. A plain plate shoe interferes least with a horse's way of going, partly because it's lighter than a shoe with a toe grab or heel calks. A shoe with creases for the nails gives a little better traction than plate shoes, in which the nail holes are merely punched. In some instances, however, a horse used for athletic purposes needs better traction than a plate shoe gives. In the mountains a horse may need some buildup at the toe and heel for better traction on rocks and slippery hillsides. Even a grassy side hill can be too slippery for a horse wearing plates, and he may fall down.

Horses that work at speed on various types of surfaces need appropriate traction to perform without risk of falling. In these cases the activity should dictate the proper type of traction. A horse needs enough traction to travel safely and work at peak performance but not so much that the hoof grabs the ground and stops abruptly. Too much traction hinders the hoof's ability to slide. The abrupt grab not only increases shock and concussion but also can cause injuries

Toe grabs, heel calks, and nail creases provide extra traction.

due to the jerk and strain on joints, ligaments, and tendons. The horse needs enough traction to prevent slipping and falling, straining joints, or pulling muscles while scrambling — yet not so much that unnatural stress is put on his legs. Many types of traction devices increase concussion because less surface area hits the ground.

Other kinds of traction devices can be injurious as well. Borium, calks, studs, etc., should be used with care because too much traction can tear ligaments and break legs. These special devices are best used only for specific situations, such as slow work on ice, jumping on wet grass, or racing on certain types of precarious track surfaces or some other type of slippery footing. In these instances removable calks are handy.

Shoe design can increase or decrease traction. A flat, wide-webbed shoe with a beveled edge that doesn't cut into the ground much will give the least traction while a shoe with a sharp edge or a rim shoe will cut into the ground more and give better traction. Polo plates are rim shoes with a higher inside rim to give traction while still enabling the foot to have a flexible and rapid breakover.

The following types of traction devices are often used:

1. Various types of toe or heel elevation.

2. Toe grabs on the front of the shoe in various heights: low (projecting 2 millimeters into ground surface); regular (3 millimeters); and Quarter Horse type (4 millimeters).

3. Studs or calks may be part of the shoe or added to it. Blocked calks are large and square; swelled calks are rounded.

Screw-in calks or studs can be put on or taken off — with different sizes and shapes for various footing.

4. Stickers are calks used only on the outside heel of a hind shoe — for traction or to straighten the foot as it lands.

5. Spots of borium are welded to the shoe.

6. Rim shoes have a groove that fills with dirt, running all around the shoe; dirt on dirt has more traction than steel on dirt.

BORIUM

If a horse wears out shoes faster than his feet grow (as some endurance horses and other hard-working horses will), you can add material to the wearing surfaces to make them last longer. Borium (tungsten carbide, used on bits for drilling through solid rock) is often used for this purpose and can be spot-welded to the shoe. Contained in small-diameter steel rods, these crystals of tungsten carbide are very sharp and hard as diamonds. When the rods are welded to a steel shoe, the outer material melts and bonds with the shoe while the crystals retain their sharp edges. The resulting rough surface is harder than steel and will not wear away. It also gives good traction on rocks, concrete, ice, and other slippery surfaces.

Borium should be added to the wear points — a spot on each heel and a spot on each side of the toe — the four basic points of natural hoof contact. Putting the borium on each side of the toe (rather than the front of the toe) can help the foot to break over center, correcting a horse with a mild crookedness of foot flight — making the foot start its flight straight. This is often the simplest solution for a horse

Borium spots can make shoes last longer.

that tends to swing his foot inward and interfere due to improper breakover.

A shoe with spots of borium added to the wear points may last up to 10 times as long as an ordinary shoe. It may have to be reset periodically as the hoof grows, but it will not wear out before the horse needs to be reshod. If the shoe is reset many times, however, the nail holes tend to get bigger (from nail wear) and must be "necked" down or reduced to avoid movement.

WINTER TRACTION

Calks or studs are often used for winter riding but are not good for all surfaces. On rocks or pavement, calks may slip and can actually create poor traction; there isn't enough shoe surface contacting the hard ground. Borium gives better traction on frozen ground than calks or studs. When choosing a specific type of traction for winter shoes, you don't want too much grip or the horse's feet and legs may suffer strain. The horse needs a little bit of give and slide (as he naturally has on dirt or grass) to avoid excessive strain or concussion. The foot's coming to a complete halt the instant it touches the ground, ice, or pavement may produce too much trauma — resulting in strains and sprains or even broken bones.

In winter, snow may pack in the foot of a shod horse and become a ball of ice, creating very hazardous footing. Snow tends to pack in a shod hoof more than it does in a bare foot; the shoe holds snow, hindering the self-cleaning action of the foot. Under these conditions greasing the bottom of the feet with butter, margarine, petroleum jelly, or some other non-stick material such as Pam (which doesn't spray on very well in cold weather) or ski wax (which stays on the foot longer than anything else) helps keep snow from sticking to the sole.

Snow pads can also be used to keep the snow from building up in the foot. There are two types of snow pads. One is flat across the foot with a protruding bubble that pops the snow out of the foot. The other is basically a rim pad that leaves frog and sole exposed, but the pad encircles the shoe with a lip that keeps the snow from sticking to the shoe. You still have the traction effect of the frog, with less ice buildup in the foot.

CHAPTER 6

Dealing with Loose or Lost Shoes

Horses occasionally lose shoes or their shoes become loose and must be removed or tightened if it is not yet time for a reshoeing. If a horse loses shoes frequently, the cause must be discovered and corrected.

REASONS FOR LOST SHOES

Some horses repeatedly lose shoes because of poor hoof walls that won't hold nails or because of the way they travel — stepping on the heel of a front shoe with the hind foot and pulling the shoe off. A lost shoe leaves a hoof vulnerable to damage. Losing a shoe may also tear part of the hoof wall away.

Some shoes are lost accidentally, such as a horse catching a shoe while backing out of a trailer, pawing a wire fence and catching the heel, or getting the heel hooked over the bottom rail of a metal gate. Sometimes the horse pulls off a shoe that alters his natural gait. Heavy shoes, for instance, increase leg swing and stride and may cause a horse to over-reach. Studs or calks may change the stride enough to create problems. A tired horse may not travel as correctly as a fit and energetic horse; if a horse becomes too fatigued on a long ride, he may start hitting himself because his strides are more wobbly. He may also step on himself.

Wet conditions can soften the hoof wall, spreading the hoof and loosening the clinches. Exposure to alternating dryness and moisture can dry out hooves, just as human hands can be when they are constantly in and out of water. Weather that alternates from wet to dry to wet can repeatedly expand and contract the hoof wall, making the foot more brittle and cracked. A hoof may deteriorate so much that it's hard to find a solid place to hold a nail.

Horsemen often blame mud for pulling off shoes, but the actual culprit may be the moisture that softens hooves so they don't hold nails well. Deep footing can hinder a horse's balance and stride. A horse struggling through a bog, for example, can step on himself, pulling the shoe off. Horses that run and play on wet, slippery footing can also grab a shoe.

> ## AT A GLANCE
>
> Common causes for losing a shoe:
>
> - Stepping on it with another foot.
> - Catching it on something.
> - Scrambling or floundering through boggy, wet footing.
> - Crumbly hoof walls that won't hold nails.
> - Hooves too soft.
> - Shoes and nails worn out.
> - Overlong or unbalanced feet.

Conformation can play a role, too. A base-narrow horse may occasionally step on a front foot with his other front (if the shoe projects past the hoof in the heel and quarters) just because his feet stand so close together.

A horse with long hind legs or a horse with a short back and long legs may forge, pulling off front shoes. Young horses sometimes forge and hit their front and hind shoes together, partly because they are still unbalanced with a rider, are not yet fit enough to handle themselves with agility, or are still taller at the croup.

Shoes left on too long are often lost. A long-toed hind foot delays and hinders breakover, resulting in a longer stride and the potential for the hind foot to hit the front foot and pull off a shoe. If the long hoof overgrows the shoe at the heels

A lost shoe can cause problems.

and quarters, placing undue weight on the hoof wall, the wall tends to collapse or break and the clinches come loose. Once the shoe is loose at the heels, it may rotate and twist, making it susceptible to being stepped on by another foot. Sometimes the nail heads wear off completely, or the nails break and the shoe just falls off.

Many horse owners do not time shoeing to match the growth rate of their horses' feet and shoes stay on too long. This can be a problem if one horse on the farm needs a five-week shoeing interval while another individual can go eight or nine weeks. Unless you do your own shoeing and can shoe each horse at the optimum moment, timing your farrier's visits to coincide with each horse's needs can be difficult.

PULLING A SHOE

If you do your own shoeing, you need to learn how to pull off a shoe with the least stress to the horse's hoof and joints. But even if a farrier does your shoeing, you should still learn how to pull a shoe properly for situations that require prompt attention to avoid injury to your horse. If the shoe is hanging loose on one side or at risk of catching on something or causing a corn or bruise because it has slipped, it needs to come off. Having the shoe accidentally pulled off may break the hoof wall or take a chunk out of the hoof, making the foot harder to reshoe.

A shoe is easy to remove without breaking the hoof wall if you have a few shoeing tools or adequate substitutes. A shoeing hammer, clinch cutter, nippers, and rasp will make the job easy, but you can also use a flat-edged screwdriver instead of a clinch cutter and a regular carpenter's hammer if necessary. Hoof cutters or pulling nippers are best for pulling a shoe, but if you don't have these and the shoe is fairly loose, you can use a pair of vice grips or even regular pliers to hold onto the shoe and give you some leverage.

The shoe is easiest to remove and you are less likely to break off hoof wall if you first un-clinch the remaining nails. Cut the clinched nails on the hoof wall with a clinch cutter or unbend them with hoof nippers. To pry up the clinch and straighten it out, use any kind of hammer to drive the clinch cutter or use a flat screwdriver under each nail end. This method may be easiest with the horse's foot on the ground. If using a carpenter's hammer, remember that it is heavier than a shoeing hammer; be careful not to hit the hoof too hard. Hold the hammer closer to the head (choking up the handle) to make sure you use lighter taps. If using a screwdriver, be careful not to cut into the hoof wall. Once each nail is unclinched, cut off the straightened nail end with nippers.

If you don't have a clinch cutter, nippers, or screwdriver, rasp off the clinched nail ends with a rasp or file. Rest the

---

AT A GLANCE

To pull a shoe:

• Hold the foot in shoeing position and place the pulling pincers or nippers (or vice grips) between the shoe and hoof at the heel.

• To make the job easier, start at the heel, where the shoe is loosest.

• Close the handle of the pincers or vice grips and push it away from you to loosen the heel branch of the shoe, pushing slightly toward the middle line of the foot. Always push the tool's handle toward the center of the sole; prying outward may tear off a chunk of hoof wall with the shoe.

• Use downward force to pry and loosen the shoe.

• Work alternately along each branch, moving toward the toe as the shoe comes loose.

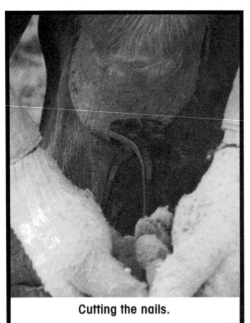

Cutting the nails.

horse's foot on your knee and rasp each clinch until the clinch is gone or can no longer hold. Then you can pull the shoe easily. Slip the claws of a carpenter's hammer under the heel of the shoe. Push the head of the hammer toward the frog to pry the shoe at the heel. Then slowly work the claws around the shoe until it comes off.

If you have shoeing tools, use pulling pincers or old hoof cutters to pull the shoe. It's better to pull it than just cut the nails (between shoe and hoof) as some people do. Cutting the nails will dull the tool and leave nail pieces in the hoof wall. They must be removed after the shoe is off. Pulling out nail pieces with nippers, pliers, or pincers afterward is much more likely to break or crack the horse's hoof wall than pulling the shoe properly.

As you pull the shoe loose, hold the foot securely and do not twist the pincers or pull crookedly so as not to strain or injure the fetlock joint. The horse will protest if you twist the joint. Continue working down both branches alternately until the entire shoe is loosened. Remove each nail as it's loosened.

If you have been unable to undo the clinches or rasp them off, removing the shoe as described will take more strength and leverage — as the shoe itself must pull the clinches loose and through the hoof wall. As you pull the shoe away from the foot, the nails will straighten and come off with the shoe. If some of the clinches are still fairly tight, however, the hoof wall may break as you pop off the shoe unless you take each nail out as you go. It is important to remove each nail as the shoe is loosened.

To get hold of a nail head with hoof pincers or pliers, you

may have to pound the loosened shoe gently back down against the hoof so the loosened nail head protrudes enough to grasp with nippers, pliers, or hammer claws. Take that nail out; then, pull on the shoe again to loosen it enough to take out the next nail, alternating down each side of the shoe. If a nail has broken off in the hoof wall, after you have removed the shoe, grasp the nail with nippers or pliers to pull it out. Don't leave pieces of nail in the wall. If they stick out, the horse may injure himself (or you) with them.

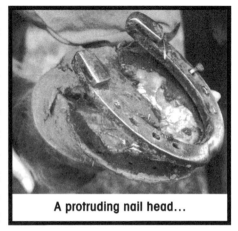

A protruding nail head...

...makes it easier to remove.

TIGHTENING A LOOSE SHOE

Check the security of the shoes every time you groom the horse or clean the feet. Definitely check them before every ride. After you clean the foot, try wiggling the shoe branches with your fingers or prying gently under the heel of each branch with the hoof pick. If the shoe moves, it needs tightening.

If a shoe is a little loose because of loose clinches but not yet in real danger of falling off, tighten the clinches to keep the shoe from becoming completely loose. This may be adequate to keep the shoe secure for a few more days until you or your farrier can reshoe the horse.

It is not wise to leave the shoe clanking; there's more risk of losing it and part of the hoof wall with it. Also, movement on the loose clinches will enlarge the nail holes and weaken the surrounding hoof horn and may wear some of the nails in two. If the shoe gets any looser, it may shift position on the foot. Also, the loose clinches may stick out from the hoof wall, increasing the horse's likelihood of hitting himself .

If you have to ride the horse before you can schedule a reshoeing or if he has weak hoof walls and you don't want him barefoot for fear of the hoof's cracking or breaking, you may not want to take the shoe off just yet; it's better to re-clinch it. Merely tapping the protruding clinches down with a hammer is unwise as this may just roll them under and damage the hoof wall. The balled-up clinch still sticks out and could nick another leg.

To do a good job reclinching, you must straighten the old clinch first. If you don't have farrier's tools, you can substitute a hammer and screwdriver. Once you've straightened the clinch, cut the long end off with clinch cutters, hoof nippers, or even by rasping it a little. Also, rasp a new notch under the protruding nail tip. Then reclinch the nail by placing any square-edged piece of metal (even the side of a rasp) against the tip of the nail that is still protruding from the hoof wall. Tap the nail head down firmly again into the shoe crease. Your metal edge turns the nail as you pound it down.

Once you've hammered the nail, use a clinching tool to squeeze the nail tip over tightly, pushing it down into the small groove you've made with the rasp. If you don't have a clinching tool, hold a piece of metal against the nail head while you pound the clinch over into the groove with your hammer; then pound it down more completely while the horse is standing with his foot on the ground. The retightened clinch(es) should hold until the shoe is ready to be replaced.

If a lost nail needs to be replaced, use the same nail hole (unless the hoof wall is broken out at that location) and care-fully tap the new nail in and clinch it. It's better not to make another hole in the hoof wall; you or your farrier will appre-ciate less weakening of the wall when you have to reshoe the horse. Make sure the nail hole is free of dirt and debris. Tapping on the shoe with a hammer will usually dislodge any dirt in the hole. If a piece of broken-off nail is still in the hole or you can't clear the old hole, don't put in another nail.

OUT ON THE TRAIL

Occasionally, a shoe comes loose on a ride but is still hanging on. You may hear it clanking as you travel on pavement, rocks, or firm ground. Stop immediately and assess whether it will stay on until you get home or whether the shoe needs emergency tightening or removal.

It's wise to carry a pocket (or belt-loop) tool that serves as a knife, screwdriver, and pliers. With this type of tool, you can do emergency repairs on tack, tighten a loose shoe, or pull one off that is dangling. You might be able to retighten the clinches enough to keep the shoe on until you get home if you can straighten them with your pocket-tool screwdriver and bend them down again with a rock.

If the shoe is dangling or one side is loose, remove the shoe so it won't catch on something and pull off or injure the other leg should the shoe twist out of position. Be careful not to tear off any hoof wall with the shoe. With your pocket tool you can pry any clinches that are still holding, straightening them or pulling the nails out so the shoe can be more easily pulled off without damaging the wall. If you just wrestle the shoe off, you nearly always tear away some of the hoof wall where the clinches were still holding.

PROTECTING THE FOOT AFTER LOSING A SHOE

If you are riding a horse that loses his shoe, you may have to improvise a way to protect the foot before you can get home. His feet are not very tough because the shoe protected the vulnerable areas. Even if the hoof wall is not damaged when the shoe comes off, the edge of the wall can soon chip and crack. The horse that just lost his shoe may also suffer a stone bruise or become tenderfooted if you travel through rocky country or on gravel roads to get home.

If the shoe is still dangling, remove it carefully, if you can, and try not to tear off any hoof wall. A hoof boot is the ideal solution for getting him safely home, but most riders don't carry these, especially if their horse seldom loses a shoe. Endurance riders and many trail riders often carry an Easyboot or some other type of protective boot (Old Macs work about the best) along with them for such emergencies. The boot can protect the bare foot until the ride ends or a farrier becomes available.

But what kind of hoof protection can a rider improvise in the middle of nowhere? A sweater, sweatshirt, or light jacket can be folded to use as padding, tying the sleeves around the foot and pastern to hold it in place. This may enable you to lead the horse home without damaging the foot further.

Because it might be a day or two before the horse can be reshod, put on a more effective hoof cover when you get home. Clean the foot and use a protective boot, or apply duct tape over the bottom of the foot and around the lower portion of the hoof wall to pad the edges. If the horse's foot is tender, add more protection, such as a hoof pad or folded towel, taped to the bottom of the foot. If the horse is in a stall or dry paddock and not being ridden, this temporary protection will suffice until he can be shod.

WAYS TO PREVENT LOOSE SHOES

If a horse repeatedly pulls off front shoes by stepping on them with his hind feet, your farrier may have to shoe him differently; the hind shoes may need to be more squared at the toe to prevent contact with the heels of the front shoes. Rolled or rocker toes on the front shoes can help the horse pick up his front feet a little more quickly and easily to avoid the approaching hind feet. A horse ordinarily shod for maximum support might have to forgo an extra-long heel so less shoe protrudes. The trauma of having the shoe ripped off may damage the hoof more than shoeing it closely.

Some horses that consistently jerk off front shoes by stepping on the heels with the hind feet — especially during speed work and competition — can be helped by using bell boots on the front feet. The boots come down far enough to cover the heel area and keep the toe of the hind foot from grabbing the heel of the front shoe. If a horse loses shoes when running out in the pasture, however, bell boots may not be a solution because you may not want to leave the boots on the horse full time.

Before a horse is shod, his use, environment, and hoof health must be carefully weighed. Some farriers are purists about shoeing the foot exactly right for proper support and hoof expansion. They will use a corrective shoe that sticks out for some purpose or small-diameter nails and short clinches that will pull out easily without breaking the hoof wall.

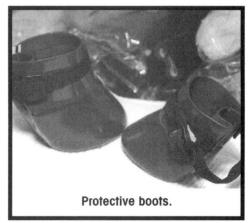

Protective boots.

This is fine in many instances, but not for the horse whose work makes a lost shoe a disaster. In these situations, especially when the hoof is reasonably sound and healthy to begin with, it is better to fit the shoe closer to the foot and use longer and sturdier clinches that won't easily loosen.

If a farrier shoes your horse, and too many shoes are coming off, you and your farrier should carefully evaluate the problem and devise a solution. Your farrier may need to try some other options: lighter shoes, different type or number of nails, different placement of clinches, clips to help hold the shoe on, ways to aid or impede breakover of certain feet to make sure the shoes don't meet, etc. If you and the farrier cannot agree on a modified approach to reduce the incidence of shoe loss on a problem horse, try a different farrier.

CHAPTER 7

Common Foot Problems

Most hoof problems result from poor living conditions, inadequate nutrition, improper shoeing, or genetics. Not every horse is blessed with ideal feet; some inherit thin soles or hoof walls, small feet, crooked legs, or low heels, for example. In most instances, though, a horseman can prevent serious problems with proper shoeing, good care, a dry environment, and diligent efforts to correct small problems before they become large ones.

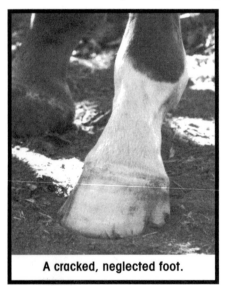

A cracked, neglected foot.

THRUSH

Thrush is a type of hoof rot, characterized by black necrotic (dead) tissue in the cleft and grooves of the frog and sometimes the sole of the foot (especially near the white line). It is caused by pathogenic organisms found in barnyards, stables, or pastures. These organisms thrive in wet or decaying material such as mud or manure.

Several pathogens can cause thrush, but most common is *Fusobacterium necrophorum*, bacteria that can also cause foot rot in cattle, diphtheria in calves, and navel (joint) ill in foals and calves. Because the pathogens prefer a damp, dark, airless environment, deep grooves along the frog make an ideal habitat, especially if the hoof is always packed with dirt, mud, or manure. The lack of air next to the frog and the constant moisture work together to allow the infection to flourish. A horse kept in a wet, boggy pasture; muddy pen; or dirty stall is more likely to develop thrush than a horse kept in a dry, clean pasture or a clean stall. A hoof that is always clean and dry won't develop thrush.

> ## AT A GLANCE
>
> Common foot problems include:
> - Thrush
> - Contracted heels
> - Flat feet
> - White line disease
> - Laminitis
> - Navicular syndrome
> - Hoof cracks
> - Sole bruises
> - Corns

Improper trimming and shoeing and poor hoof health can make a frog more susceptible to thrush. Horses with contracted feet have deep clefts along the frog; dirt and manure can accumulate there. Frequently cleaning all the material from the frog and its clefts helps prevent thrush. Torn or ragged pieces of frog should be trimmed as they are no longer useful to the horse's foot and provide nooks and crevices where thrush could start. A properly trimmed frog won't collect mud and debris so readily. Regular exercise on dry ground also is good prevention. Flexing of the foot (expanding and contracting) as the horse travels enables the lodged material to fall out. If feet can dry out and air can get to all parts of the hoof, thrush won't get started.

Thrush is easily recognized by the dark color along the frog (and sometimes dark soft patches in the sole, especially along the white line), and by the strong, offensive smell of the foot. A black, slimy moisture in the clefts of the frog tends to stick to a hoof pick when you clean the foot.

When the clefts are cleaned out, you will notice they are deeper than normal and may extend into sensitive tissues; therefore, the horse may flinch as they are cleaned because there is not much tissue between your hoof pick and sensitive tissue. The frog may be undermined with infection, and large areas of it may be loose. Loose tags should be removed. If thrush is neglected and allowed to worsen, it can make the horse lame. The infection can spread and erode more of the foot.

Thrush in its early stages can be easily cleared up by cleaning the feet and then applying an astringent disinfectant such as tincture of iodine, copper sulfate, chlorine bleach (equal parts bleach and water), or a thrush medication such as Kopertox to the affected area daily for a few days. Remove all debris with a hoof pick; then scrub the frog and its grooves with an old toothbrush and soap and water. Dry the foot thoroughly before applying the medication. Whatever chemical you use, be careful not to spill any on the horse's skin or on other parts of the hoof as it may burn the skin and dry out the hoof. Treating the foot just once won't cure thrush, nor will periodic applications if the horse's feet are continually packed with mud or manure between treatments, so be sure to keep the feet clean and dry.

If thrush is well started before it's discovered, large areas of the frog may have to be trimmed and the foot may have sustained permanent damage. If infection has entered sensitive tissues, the area should be cleaned, opened for drainage, and the horse given antibiotics under veterinary supervision. Thrush that has invaded the inner tissues should be treated like an infected puncture wound — with a tetanus shot, antibiotics, and daily cleaning and soaking of the foot (described later in this chapter) to help pull infection out of the tissues. The foot should be bandaged between soakings to keep dirt out until the inner tissues have healed. The cleft of the frog can be packed with cotton soaked in iodine when you reapply bandages to the foot.

CANKER

Another problem that occasionally affects a frog and sole in wet climates is necrotic pododermatitis or "canker." This infectious condition results in abnormal growth of horn, sometimes creating a white to yellowish mound of soft material with a foul smell. Treatment consists of removing the abnormal tissue and topical application of metronidazole or chloramphenicol (strong antibiotics). The affected area may need trimming more than once during the healing process to make sure the daily medication can get to the infection, as abnormal tissue may regrow. It may take two to 12 weeks to halt canker completely.

INFECTION BETWEEN THE HEEL BULBS

Inflammation of the skin between the bulbs of the heel often occurs in horses with contracted heels, where the heel bulbs grow closer together and a deep crevice forms between them. Moisture and dirt in this crevice can lead to a painful infection. It smells and looks like thrush — in fact, the same organism may cause the infection — so some horsemen treat it like thrush. However, using iodine or other harsh chemicals (typically used for thrush) on the infected skin can cause a chemical burn that worsens the condition.

To treat a thrush-like infection between the heel bulbs, clean and dry the affected area; then saturate a few gauze strips with a suitable antibiotic salve and work the medicated strips — one at a time — down into the groove between the heel bulbs. The protruding ends of the strips can be cut off. Each day the old strips should be removed and newly medicated strips inserted. After a few days the space between the bulbs will widen a bit and the infection will clear up.

If the heels are contracted due to improper shoeing, this situation should be corrected.

CONTRACTED FEET

Contracted heels or feet have been traditionally classed as

unsoundness in a horse. Even if the horse is not lame, this condition may make him more likely to go lame because of the foot's inability to absorb and dissipate concussion adequately. A horse with this problem is more susceptible to heel pain or concussion-related injuries.

Front feet are normally quite round, and hind feet more narrow and concave at the sole. A contracted foot is narrower than normal, especially at the heels and quarters. The frog shrinks to the point it no longer contacts the ground. Contraction is more common in front feet than hind, especially if caused by improper shoeing. Sometimes only one foot is contracted due to injury and lameness.

Even though some breeds' feet are conformed more oval than round, their feet are not contracted. Construction and health of heels, bars, sole, and frog can help you differentiate between a normal, healthy narrow foot and a contracted one. In some horses one front foot is narrower as an inherited condition; it may or may not cause problems. The true contracted foot is a pathological condition in which important structures have degenerated.

Foot expansion is essential to foot health. Contraction is a result of breakdown in the shock absorption mechanisms of the foot; the hoof has lost its ability to compress in height and expand in width when it takes weight, and it becomes smaller. It's a vicious cycle; once contraction begins, foot function is badly impaired and the condition becomes worse. Once a foot is badly contracted, it may take several careful trimmings/shoeings to become normal again.

A dished or concave sole often accompanies foot contraction. Because the heels can't expand, the foot no longer flattens when weight is placed on it. The sole arches upward. If contraction becomes severe, the hoof wall may press against the coffin bone inside the foot, making the horse lame (hoof bound). The frog of a contracted foot is often an inch or more above the ground. Heels may be so narrow and close together that the bars of the foot actually touch one another.

The sole, frog, and even the hoof wall may become very hard, dry, and difficult to trim. The coffin bone may become deformed. The digital cushion above the frog tends to shrink and atrophy — becoming less resilient — losing its protective buffering action for the deep flexor tendon and navicular bone. Corrective trimming and shoeing can often reverse contraction (see Chapter 8), but the primary cause should be discovered and corrected. If feet are hard and dry, efforts should be made to restore moisture to the hoof.

FLAT FEET AND HOOF PADS

If you have a flat-footed horse that bruises easily, shoe him protectively early in the riding season before he bruises or gets tenderfooted. Once he bruises, he may be lame for weeks. The area most vulnerable to bruising is the front part of the sole, right behind the toe. Pads can prevent trouble before it starts. Many flat-footed or thin-soled horses get into the habit of shortening their stride in rocks or gravel, but with adequate hoof protection they no longer move with hesitation.

Flat feet tend to bruise or become tender more readily than feet with normal, concave soles. A flat-footed horse that is well shod and never used in rocky terrain may not become tender, but he may go lame if ridden on gravel roads or rocks.

Horses with flat feet or thin soles, or horses that have suffered from laminitis or dropped soles, may need added protection. The flat-footed horse's sole is on the ground, subjecting the sensitive tissues above it to jarring or bruising if the horse hits a rock. If the inner tissues bruise badly enough, a hoof abscess may develop and cause pain (from pressure inside the hoof) and lameness. A hoof abscess can lay up a horse for several weeks or months, especially if the sole must be drained and new horn grown to fill the hole. A deep bruise, even if it does not abscess, may take weeks to heal.

Hoof pads can protect a thin or flat sole and prevent stone bruising, but if you only ride occasionally on rocky ground, hoof boots may be preferable. Sized properly, hoof boots can be put on over shoes or bare feet when your horse is traveling in rocks and then removed when footing is softer.

If you use hoof pads, the pad goes between the hoof and the shoe when the shoe is nailed on. A frequently ridden horse needs something more durable than some of the commercial pads. Most of the cushion pads (used to minimize concussion) will wear through before it's time to reshoe the horse. The shock-absorbing pads are fine for a horse recovering from founder, a horse with arthritic joints, navicular disease, and other problems associated with concussion, but they are inadequate for the horse needing durable protection in the rocks. Synthetic shoe-sole material, the neoprene used by shoe-repair shops, works better and lasts as long as a steel horseshoe. Large sheets, which provide enough material for many hoof pads, can be purchased from a shoe shop. Most flat-footed horses only need pads in front. Hind feet are usually more concave and do not carry as much weight; therefore, they are rarely flat and seldom bruise.

If you decide to use a neoprene pad, first shape the shoe to fit the foot perfectly, then trace around it for the size and shape of the hoof pad. Cut out the pad with a sharp knife or a pad cutter. The finished, slick side should be the ground surface because that side wears longer. When attaching the shoe (with pad between it and the hoof), you must drive the nails an extra 1/4-inch to allow for the depth of the pad under the shoe.

For a normal, non-flat hoof any space between the sole and pad is filled with silicone rubber calking or a medicated hoof-packing compound. A truly flat foot doesn't need any filling, except for the space right next to the frog — if you use a regular pad that covers the entire foot, frog and all. Putting a pad over the entire foot of a flat-footed horse will be difficult because the pad must bend up over the frog; the frog sticks out beyond the flat sole. You'll have better luck leaving out the packing or filler and shaping the pad to cover just the sole. Cut out a wedge-shaped portion so the pad does not cover the frog at all. Thus, the frog is open to the air and stays healthier, making the bottom of the foot less prone to thrush. The pad lies perfectly flat on the flat sole, with no bending and no gaps to fill. The foot also has more traction on grass than it would with the whole bottom covered.

If you cut away the area to accommodate the frog, filler is unnecessary. The soles of some horses' feet might have slight irregularities, but the spaces are small enough to pack with a little bit of cotton. Putting the pad and shoe on straight and in the proper location is easier when the frog isn't covered because you can still use the frog as a guide for centering the shoe on the foot.

A horse with pads does not get much air next to the sole. If he's in a wet pasture or muddy pen, moisture may get trapped under the pad, keeping his sole wet and creating ideal conditions for thrush. A hoof packed with silicone also may get moisture next to the foot; the silicone won't keep it out. To prevent or halt a case of thrush under a pad, apply iodine. You can use a small syringe to squirt it under the pad. This is less messy than trying to pour it between pad and sole, and you are less apt to spill any on you or the horse (which tends to "burn" the skin). Hold the foot up so iodine from the syringe will flow under the pad, covering the sole. Thrush is not usually a problem if you've cut out an area for the frog and didn't have to pack the foot; that part of the foot can stay clean and dry, exposed to the air. If you keep a horse padded all season, put iodine under the pads occasionally. Using it too often, however, may corrode the shoe nails.

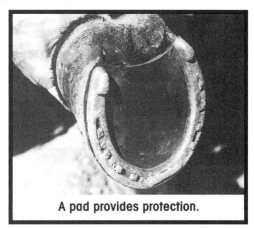

A pad provides protection.

TOUGHENING TENDER FEET

Some horses are borderline on whether they need hoof pads and can be protected from getting tender feet by regular use of iodine on the soles. Tincture of iodine acts as an astringent and helps toughen soles and makes them less sensitive. Some horses are not good candidates for hoof pads because they tend to trip if toes or feet are longer than normal. Anything that adds to foot length (even the pad) may be a problem. It's better to try to get by without pads by using iodine instead. This also works well for any freshly trimmed or newly shod horse that might be tender for a few days. Part of the sole may be soft after trimming, and it needs to toughen up again. Applying iodine a time or two before you start riding him over rocks may prevent tenderfootedness.

BRUISES AND CORNS

Trauma to the inner tissues of the foot beneath the horny sole can rupture small blood vessels, creating a bruise. When the horse steps on a sharp rock, for instance, the crushing of blood vessels between the sole and the coffin bone causes bleeding; the pressure buildup can create a lot of pain. The horse may be reluctant to put weight on the foot.

A mild bruise may merely produce tenderness; the horse may travel fine on soft ground but limp on gravel or rocks. The hard surfaces put more pressure on the sore spot. A mild sole bruise may make him short-strided or unsteady in his efforts to walk more lightly on the sore foot. With time the foot may heal on its own. If the horse continues to walk on hard surfaces that affect the sore area, the bruise could become worse.

A heel bruise will make the horse put more weight on the toe. A horse with a bruise in the toe area will land on the heel. Hoof testers (see Chapter 9) can be helpful in locating the bruise; the horse will flinch when the bruised area is pressed. If the tender part of the sole is pared down a little with a hoof knife, a reddish or bluish discoloration may be visible. Spots or streaks of blood in the bruised area look fresh even if the bruise occurred days or weeks earlier; the blood in the sole tissue has been protected from breakdown because it was encased in horn and not exposed to air.

A horse with shallow or flat feet or extremely long toes may get a bruise near the tip of the frog, especially if the edge of the coffin bone bruises the inner sole. A sharp rock can create a bruise anywhere on the sole. In some thin-soled horses, bruising may become chronic, eventually causing inflammation of the coffin bone (and permanent lameness). The coffin bone is only about three-eighths of an inch away from the sole in a normal foot, so a thin sole doesn't give it much protection. The sole can also be compromised (becoming too soft) from too much moisture or bathing. Just as washing dishes long enough can soften fingernails to the point of bending, detergent shampoos can weaken the horn. A soft or brittle sole bruises more easily. Horses shod to correct a gait problem or to straighten a foot or leg may be trimmed excessively in an attempt to balance the foot. Excessive trimming puts more pressure on one area and may cause bruising. A sole trimmed too deeply may make it more susceptible to bruising.

A bruise at the angle of the bars (where hoof wall and bars meet) is called a corn. Corns are often caused by shoes being too narrow or left on too long. Sometimes a farrier bends the inside branch of the shoe (at the heel) in toward the frog to keep the horse's hind foot from stepping on the back of the front shoe. An imperfectly fitted shoe may create direct pressure on the sole at the angle of the bars (instead of on the hoof wall), and repeated concussion in this vulnerable area may cause bruising. Use of a shoe too small for the foot can also increase pressure on the sole in this area, and heel calks can aggravate this effect.

A push corn occurs when an upright or pinched heel puts too much weight directly on sensitive heel tissues. A shoe left on too long can cause a bruised heel, especially if the hoof wall starts to grow down around the outside of the shoe. This puts pressure inside the hoof wall at the bars and crushes the tissues near the back corner of the coffin bone. A toe that is too long can cause a pull corn by putting extra leverage and stress on some parts of the hoof wall at each step. The leverage stress injures the juncture where the horny sole meets the sensitive laminae inside the foot.

Bruising can also can occur in the hoof wall — if the hoof strikes a rock (or a fence rail when jumping) or kicks a solid object. A bruise in the wall is easily visible in a non-pigmented hoof but not a dark one. A red stain in the white line (usually discovered later when trimming the foot) indicates a past injury that is growing out.

A serious bruise may abscess and require treatment — opening and draining the abscess, soaking the foot, and applying iodine. Once drained and treated, an abscess usually resolves quickly, but the hole in the sole may take several months to fill with new horn. During that time the horse is vulnerable to re-injury whenever he travels on rocky or uneven ground, and he should not be ridden unless the hole can be covered with a special shoe to protect it. A hoof pad is usually not enough protection if he travels on gravel or rocks. If the hole is just behind the toe, a farrier can add some extra metal to a steel shoe to cover the hole.

A sole bruise is vulnerable to infection if there's a crack to the outside, allowing bacteria to enter. Not opening the resulting abscess so it can drain causes a lot of pain, and the abscess may eventually break out in the heel area. Heat and swelling may be present above the foot. Damage to the foot's inner structures could result if the abscess is not treated and has to travel in the foot to find a place to break out.

If the horse has become lame from an abscessed bruise, pare the sore area with a hoof knife. If there is a crack or dark spot, open it enough that the blood and serum can drain, and soak the foot to draw out any remaining infection. If you are inexperienced, have your farrier or vet open the abscessed bruise. Apply iodine after soaking; then bandage between soakings to prevent contamination of the opened area.

Antibiotics are usually not much help to a horse with a sole abscess because circulating blood does not reach this area well. The abscess is best treated locally.

Even if the infection clears up quickly, keep the foot bandaged or in a protective boot to keep out dirt until the hole begins to fill in with new horn. Once the horse walks soundly again and the area is healing, a shoe and hoof pad can keep out dirt and protect the hole in the sole until new horn grows. Or you can use a special shoe that covers the hole.

Standing a horse in crushed ice sometimes will alleviate a mild, fresh bruise and reduce swelling and inflammation. If the bruising does not create an abscess, this ice treatment may be all that's needed to relieve temporary soreness.

PUNCTURE WOUNDS IN THE FOOT

A puncture wound anywhere in the body is always serious because it can lead to tetanus. The penetrating object may introduce bacteria, and the airless environment and damaged tissue create ideal conditions for tetanus bacteria to multiply. A puncture in the foot can cause a number of problems: inner tissue damage, inflammation or fracture of the coffin bone, decay of the bone, decay of the digital cushion, and damage to the navicular bone, bursa, or deep flexor tendon. A puncture may be hard to locate if the foreign object (stick, nail) is no longer embedded. A puncture wound in the frog may not be visible; the spongy material may have closed again after the object made its hole. If the horse suddenly goes lame without any swelling in the leg, a puncture might be the cause. The horse usually gets lamer, and if the problem is not located and treated, swelling may eventually develop in the pastern or higher.

The horse's gait may indicate which area of the foot has

been punctured. The horse may try to land on the part of his foot that puts the least pressure on the punctured area. If the foot is infected, he may be reluctant to put any weight on it. A hoof tester can often help pinpoint the spot. A black spot in the sole may also be a clue and should be probed with a hoof knife to see if the spot penetrates into sensitive tissues.

If you suspect a puncture or the object is still embedded,

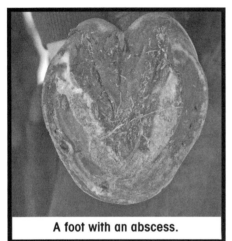

A foot with an abscess.

call your vet. Don't remove the object; the vet will have a better idea which structures might be injured (and may be able to take X-rays with the object still in place). Treatment may depend on the location and depth of the object's penetration. If the navicular bone or bursa is involved, the horse may need surgery and has a better chance of recovery if this situation is discovered at the beginning.

You may not realize the horse has stepped on something sharp until an abscess develops and he goes lame. It's best, however, to begin treatment immediately after a puncture occurs. The horse should have a tetanus shot if his booster is not recent, and antibiotics if the puncture is deep enough to cause infection that might get into the bloodstream.

If the infection has no drainage, it generally spreads until it can burst out at the coronary band. Infection from a puncture near the toe may break out near the front of the hoof; infection farther back will usually break out near the heel. If the coronary band starts draining, do not assume the injury is to the coronet. Check the bottom of the foot for a possible puncture wound, especially if the horse is lame.

"GRAVEL" INFECTION

"Gravel" is an old term for a foot infection that breaks out at the heel or coronary band after traveling upward through the hoof, causing varying degrees of lameness. Modern veterinary texts and most veterinarians will tell you the old theory about pieces of gravel migrating up through the bottom of the foot is not valid. In a barefoot horse, gravel pieces sometimes do lodge at the white line, especially if there's some separation there, but they generally do not go up into the foot. What usually happens is a crack or damaged area allows infection to invade, and if the infection goes up into the foot and no drainage is established, the pus moves to the nearest outer surface to erupt.

Because the nearest outer surface is the solid barrier of the sole or hoof wall, the infection follows the line of least resistance in the soft tissues, traveling vertically up the white line area between the sensitive and insensitive laminae and eventually breaking out at the coronary band or heel. The coronet at that spot becomes hot and swollen, and before the infection erupts it may cause lameness. When drainage begins, lameness subsides.

On rare occasion, however, gravel lameness is caused by a foreign body working upward through the hoof from the white line, such as small stones, glass shards, broken slivers of sharp flint, or even sharp plant parts such as Canadian "spear grass."

This problem rarely occurs in lightweight horses (whose hoof walls do not expand much) but can happen in heavy athletes when racing or doing fast work barefoot — such as unshod rodeo horses competing in high-speed events like roping, racing, or bulldogging. Concussion in the unshod hoof of a heavy horse doing speed work or jumping makes the hoof more susceptible to wall and sole separation at the white line, creating a vulnerable opening.

The object then migrates upward from the point of entry, traveling between the coffin bone and hoof wall in the soft tissues to come out the coronet or moving laterally beneath the coffin bone (between coffin bone and sole) to come out the heel. Painful lameness results from this migration.

Infection and pus follow the migrating object's path, but the foreign body exits the foot before the pus finds its way through the trail. The horse should get time off from work — preferably put out to pasture — to allow the infection time to break out at the heel or coronary band. More commonly, the pus that erupts is from a simple infection due to puncture or cracks that open the way for bacteria. This is a frequent cause of sudden lameness in barefoot horses at pasture.

A careful examination of white line and sole may reveal one or more black spots, which should be carefully probed to check for deeper infection and to establish drainage and get rid of the pus before it travels up through the hoof. If the problem is not caught early, opening the sole does little good; the pus pocket is too far upward. Soaking the foot can hasten the infection's rise to the surface, where it can break out and drain. The exit site may need to be enlarged and flushed out.

A poultice also can help pull infection out of the foot and can be applied by using a boot or plastic bag to hold the material next to the foot. A mixture that works well is two parts wheat bran to one part Epsom salts, in warm water, with a tablespoon of Absorbine added. The soaking boot can be left on for several days, but change the mix every 48 hours and add a couple ounces of warm water twice daily with a big syringe.

Stall rest may delay recovery because inactivity slows the upward movement of the infection. The horse is usually better off in a pen or pasture. Moving around helps the infection work up through the foot faster and erupt more quickly. A horse may wear the poultice boot while in a small pen.

Except in severe cases, most horses recover quickly, especially if the condition is discovered and treated before infection travels through the foot. Even when the pus pocket migrates to the heel or coronary band and breaks open, the horse is usually none the worse for it. Exceptions are horses with chronic laminitis; the deformed feet and dropped sole make the problem more likely to recur. Some horses that suffer long-standing gravel infections without treatment may incur permanent damage to the foot.

Prevention of "gravel" can be difficult, especially in horses at pasture, such as broodmares or retired horses, and in horses that have previously foundered. Keeping the feet smoothed and trimmed to prevent chipping and cracking, and not allowing them to become brittle, can help reduce the risk.

OPENING, DRAINING, AND SOAKING AN INFECTION

A hoof infection or abscess, whether caused by a puncture wound, infected stone bruise, deep hoof crack, neglected thrush, "gravel," or a quicked nail, usually should be drained, then soaked daily and kept bandaged until healing begins. Your vet can open the area so there is at least a 1/4-inch hole into the infected tissue for drainage.

The opened area should be flushed out with an antiseptic solution, such as 1 percent povidone iodine. If the wound does not require soaking, pack the opening with povidone iodine and bandage the foot to keep it clean and dry. If the foot needs soaking, a solution of warm water and Epsom salts (magnesium sulfate) will help pull out any remaining infection.

If the coronary band is draining, it can be flushed, using a large syringe with a long nozzle. A plastic teat cannula, such as that used to insert antibiotics into a cow's teat in treating mastitis, works well to inject the solution deep into the infection tract. The hole can be flushed once a day until the flushing no longer brings out any pus. Usually two or three days are sufficient. The foot should be kept bandaged between treatments. Once healing begins and there is no more pus, it is not as crucial to flush, soak, and bandage daily; you can do it every three or four days as healing progresses, as long as you keep the foot very clean.

If the horse has never had a foot soaked before, get him

used to the treatment gradually so it will be a good experience. Use a pliable tub, not too tall. A pliable rubber tub will harmlessly collapse if he steps on the side and will not bang his leg. Don't use a bucket with a handle. If the horse becomes nervous and quickly pulls his foot out, it may get caught in the handle.

To get your horse used to the situation, put his foot into an empty rubber tub. Once he realizes it's not scary and stands quietly, wash his foot thoroughly and put it in a clean, well-rinsed tub. Carefully add water, slightly warmer than body temperature. After he accepts it, add several tablespoonfuls of Epsom salts. Slowly pouring water into the tub while the horse is standing in it may be less alarming to him than putting his foot into an already filled tub.

Periodically add warmer water until the tub is comfortably warm (but not burning hot). Keep the water as warm as the horse can tolerate it. If he's nervous about having the foot soaked, do it at feeding time and hand-feed the horse to occupy his mind during the 30 minutes of soaking. Most horses stand quietly once they get used to the feel of the warm water; the soaking makes the foot feel better.

A soaking boot can be used if a horse won't stand with his foot in a tub. A boot is an advantage when the medication needs longer contact with the foot, and it is also handy for applying a poultice to the foot if required. The boot fits loosely on the foot, with room for the poultice material or soaking fluid to surround the foot.

Soaking a foot.

A poultice of Epsom salts and tamed iodine can be a good alternative to soaking, especially if an infection has not yet broken out. Heat applied to the foot stimulates blood flow to the in-

1) Trim the outer hoof wall with nippers.

2 & 3) Pare the sole only when necessary,
then rasp the edges smooth.

1) Fit the shoe to the foot.

2) Place nails so they enter at the white line area.

3 & 4) Keep the shoe centered
as you drive the nails.

1) Nail tips should be removed.

2) Use nail cutters or nippers to do so.

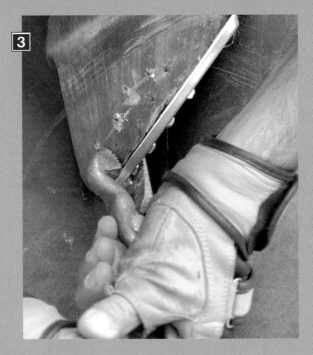

3 & 4) Clinch the nail heads, then rasp away
any rough edges.

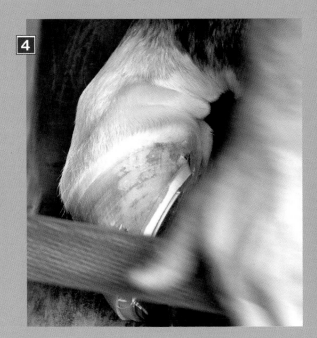

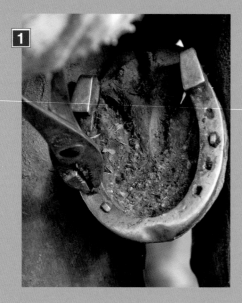

A shoe is easier to remove if you can first loosen and pull out each nail.

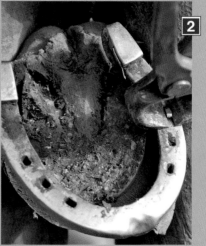

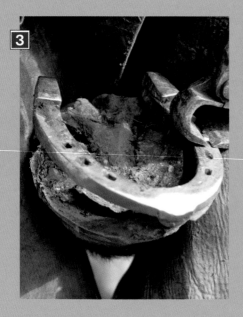

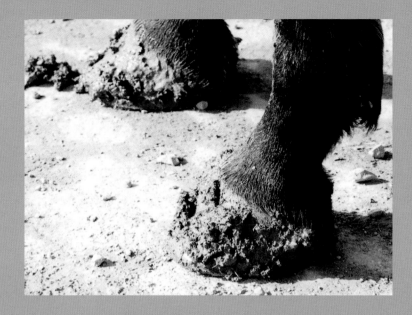

Mud is not conducive to hoof health (above) and can lead
to a variety of problems, including brittle, cracked feet
(below).

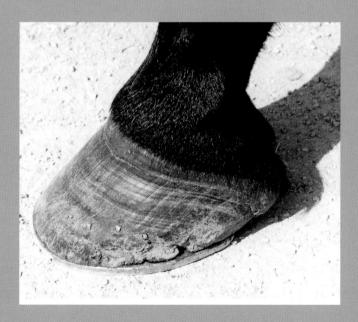

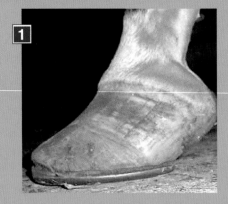

1) a hoof with chronic laminitis;

2) severe cracks that have been patched;

3) a puncture wound;

4) treating a sole with iodine.

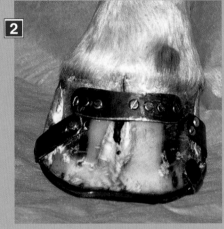

fected area, speeding up the abscess so any walled-off pockets will break open. A poultice holds the heat there longer, keeping the coronary band soft, moist, and more easily ruptured by a migrating abscess. The poultice can be changed every

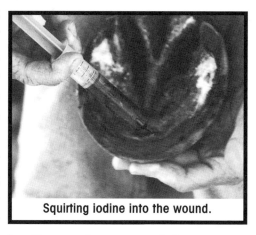

Squirting iodine into the wound.

24 to 48 hours or more often if your vet recommends it.

With some foot infections, lameness is minimal until the developing abscess creates pressure on sensitive tissues. Using hoof testers, tapping on nail heads, or tapping on the hoof wall won't reveal the area of soreness. By contrast, a horse with a pronounced lameness usually reacts to hoof testers or tapping, and the sore spot can be opened and drained. If the abscess is still in the early stages, soaking or poulticing the foot can bring the infection to a head in a few days; the horse will become much lamer and the abscess can be located and opened.

When bandaging a draining foot between soakings, dry the foot with a towel and apply a thin coat of petroleum jelly around the heel bulbs and skin above the coronary band (if soaking chaps the skin); then pack the drainage hole with cotton soaked in povidone iodine. If the hole is in the sole, pad the foot with cotton — a piece of towel or a baby diaper — then wrap the foot with stretchable bandaging material. When using stretchy tape, don't wrap any higher than the middle of the hoof wall. You can then cover the bandage with duct tape attached directly to the hoof. Finish covering the whole bandage with duct tape; it holds well and can be adequate protective covering if the ground is dry. If the footing is wet or muddy, make a smooth initial wrap (not too bulky) so the bandaged foot will fit into a waterproof boot.

CORONARY BAND INJURIES

A horse can injure the coronary band if he steps on himself or strikes himself with a shod foot, runs into something solid or sharp, or gets the foot caught in a fence or stepped on by another horse. Sometimes a horse hits his coronary band when loading or unloading from a trailer. A horse wearing studs or calks should wear bell boots when doing fast work, to protect his feet.

A veterinarian should immediately examine a deep wound at the coronet. Unless the wound is properly treated, scar tissue may disrupt the hoof's growing cells, making a weak spot in the wall that may crack easily. A large gap may disrupt hoof growth completely. A wound in the coronary band may develop proud flesh if not treated properly. Your vet can help you deal with this type of injury.

Sometimes a deep scrape or wound causes abnormal growth of skin tissue, creating a horny growth (callus) — especially if the wound is irritated by dirt, gravel, or other contaminants embedded in it. The more damaged the skin, the more risk of abnormal horn growth. Any wound to the coronet should be carefully cleaned and treated to help prevent this kind of aftermath. By the time some horny growth is evident, it is too late to treat it medically.

In some cases a scar at the coronary band causes no problem except unsightliness. If the area is healthy enough to grow normal hoof horn (not creating a weak spot that cracks), the excess horny growth can just be clipped regularly with hoof nippers to keep it flush with the coronary band. Applying a lanolin-based ointment can keep it soft and pliable — and less apt to crack and bleed.

If the growth causes pain and lameness or is struck by another foot and bleeds, a veterinarian can remove the growth surgically. If the abnormal area is completely removed down to normal tissue, it will usually heal without scar tissue, especially if the foot can be kept in a supportive bandage for two to four weeks.

HOOF CRACKS

Toe cracks, quarter cracks, and heel cracks are vertical splits between the hoof horn tubules. Those that start at ground surface are called grass cracks. Sand cracks start at the coronary band (due to defect or injury in the coronet). Sand cracks travel downward because of weakness in the wall at that area. A horizontal crack (from a blow or injury) is called a blow-out. It rarely spreads or needs treatment, but because the hoof wall is weakened at that spot, it may set the stage for a vertical crack, especially if other factors put additional stress on the hoof wall.

Cracks in the hoof wall are sometimes hard to get rid of; the hoof keeps splitting as it grows due to pressure on the crack when it bears weight. Cracks usually result from long bare feet that chip and split or result from concussion on a brittle foot or from injury. Long untrimmed feet may develop serious cracks that travel into sensitive tissue and make the horse lame. If a hoof is kept balanced, minor cracks grow out and don't become problems.

Brittle feet, caused by dry conditions, genetics, or nutrition (or a combination of these), make a horse more prone to hoof cracks. Brittleness is sometimes more common in white feet than in dark ones. If a horse has feet that crack readily, a good hoof dressing sometimes helps by reducing moisture loss in the hoof wall. Feed supplements may help if the problem is nutritional.

Quarter cracks are common in horses that have a lot of stress on feet (such as racehorses) as the quarters are the thinnest and most delicate part of the hoof wall. Quarter cracks can be due to thin walls (genetic weakness), improperly trimmed feet, concussion on hard ground, exercise on uneven ground, stones, or a misplaced shoe nail. With some horses, quarter cracks are lifelong problems; the hoof needs constant care and proper balance to keep cracks from recurring or getting worse. If a foot is brought back to balance, even a barefoot horse will grow out a bad crack — because stress on the crack has been stopped. A quarter crack usually involves a heel that's sheared; a toe crack usually involves underrun heels and too-long toes.

The element selenium also plays a role in hoof problems. A deficiency can lead to poor hoof horn whereas an excess can cause horizontal cracks. These cracks often appear near the top of the hoof, just beneath the coronary band. Excessive selenium in the body alters the normal chemical bonding of keratin that forms hoof horn. If a horse continues to eat feed containing high levels of selenium, poor hoof quality may eventually result in the wall completely separating from the foot. Usually the horse will show other signs of selenium toxicity before then, such as the horizontal hoof cracks and hair loss (especially mane and tail).

Thin hoof walls and soles make a barefoot horse susceptible to injuries, cracks, and chips. This type of hoof must be trimmed often, and the edges smoothed to help prevent chipping and cracking.

Once a foot has started splitting, growing out a bad crack on a bare foot can be difficult unless you return the foot to balance. Your farrier may decide to put on a shoe to help hold a crack together. A shoe can help keep stress off the hoof wall in that area. A clip can be put on each side of a toe crack to keep the hoof wall from expanding there when weight is put on the foot. A half bar shoe is sometimes helpful for a quarter crack; it enables the frog to bear some of the weight the wall ordinarily bears.

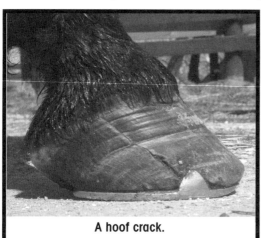

A hoof crack.

When trimming the foot in preparation for the shoe, cut away the hoof wall at the crack so it does not bear weight and expand. For a toe crack, shorten the toe. A square toe and clips can help minimize the stress during breakover. For a quarter crack or heel crack, the hoof wall at the heel should be trimmed from the crack to the back of the hoof, so heel and quarters will not take weight. Then the crack can't spread and split more. When the horse is shod, a gap is left between the shoe and the hoof wall at the crack. The weight is distributed along the rest of the shoe, with none at the crack. This allows the hoof to grow out without widening the crack.

A hoof crack originating in the coronet (due to old injury) is often a persistent problem. Special shoeing may be needed for the rest of the horse's life because the defect in the coronet weakens and distorts hoof growth. Regular use of hoof dressing can help keep the coronet and hoof wall more pliable and less apt to crack. If a crack persists in spite of careful and frequent trimming, consult your vet or farrier.

DRY, BRITTLE FEET

Hooves are healthiest when hoof horn has proper moisture levels. Tiny tubules in the hoof horn conduct moisture up and down the hoof. Dry feet often chip and crack, not having elasticity and resilience. Brittle hooves are also difficult to trim; the hoof wall may break or shatter when nippers are used. It's harder to nail a shoe securely to a dry, brittle, shelly hoof.

Some horsemen try to remedy dry feet by creating a wet spot in a pasture or paddock (next to a water tank, for instance) for horses to stand in or walk through, but this method can aggravate the problem. Being alternately wet and dry can worsen weak hooves just as repeatedly putting your hands in water dries and chaps them.

A hoof is healthiest when footing is dry, not wet, and when the horse is exercised regularly. A confined horse may not have sufficient moisture delivered to the hoof via inner blood circulation, and his feet may also contract. If a foot becomes too soft in wet weather, in mud, or through frequent bathing, the wall may spread and its layers separate. Horsemen in wet climates often protect their horses' feet with waterproof hoof dressings, sealers, and hoof hardeners.

You can't add moisture to a hoof with a dressing because hoof moisture comes from within, but you can reduce moisture loss by retaining what's already there.

Horsemen used to think mud made a good treatment for dry, cracked feet; but a hoof constantly in mud has soft walls that tend to spread, and dried mud may pull out natural oils. The worst type of moisture is urine (in dirty bedding) because ammonia breaks down the hoof horn.

When moisture evaporates through the hoof wall faster than it is replaced, the hoof dries out. A hoof sealer can help feet that are covered with tiny surface cracks caused by moisture changes. Unlike a thick, greasy dressing, a hoof sealer soaks into the hoof wall and helps keep external moisture from damaging the hoof and internal moisture from dissipating. This can help counter effects of environmental changes such as dewy pastures at night that dry out during the day or wet feet (from bathing) put into stall bedding that dries out hooves and creates cracks. To prevent excessive moisture loss, use sealant on clean, dry hooves before riding or turning out a stabled horse, making sure your horse's feet are dry after bathing him, and using good straw or shredded paper for bedding instead of wood products. Some types of shavings and sawdust dry out the feet. Greasy dressings won't help the hoof wall itself but can benefit dry and cracking heel bulbs. A product containing animal fat such as lanolin or fish oils can help restore pliability in the heels.

If a horse has very dry feet, dressings may help, but you may have to try several products to find one that works well for your horse. Read labels and follow directions. Although most hoof care products can be applied to both the wall and the coronary band, some products should be used only on the hoof. Also, follow directions for frequency of use. Applying a sealant too often may hold in too much moisture.

WHITE LINE DISEASE

White line disease is a progressive separation of the hoof wall from the foot. The disease starts at the bottom of the foot and travels upward, involving the thickest layer of hoof wall — the portion attached to the insensitive laminae. It is called white line disease only because it begins at the white line, where the sole meets the bottom of the hoof wall.

Using a hoof dressing.

The hoof horn just outside the white line is the structure affected, creating soft or chalky horn tissue. In years past, the term "seedy toe" was sometimes applied to this condition. The area of abnormal horn may only extend a short distance up from the ground surface, but usually keeps progressing upward. The material in the ever-widening space is soft and crumbly. Wall separation can begin anywhere along the bottom of the foot.

The separation may start mechanically if the hoof wall is too long. Weight placed on the foot at each step tends to pry the wall away from the sole. The opening collects dirt and manure that are forced up into this separation, making an ideal habitat for microbes that grow in hoof horn. Barefoot horses with long feet that are standing in mud may suffer wall separation due to mud or fine gravel packing into the bottom of the foot and white line area, creating a space where horn-digesting fungi become established.

The affected area expands upward along the inside of the wall toward the coronary band, creating hollow pockets filled with debris. Tapping the hoof produces a hollow sound over the affected area. A knife blade can be inserted between hoof wall and foot; if you scrape out this space, dirt and manure are usually packed in there. The hoof horn residue looks like crumbled, dry cheese. An X-ray shows a gap between hoof wall and coffin bone. In a long-standing case, the outer wall completely detaches and the coffin bone may sink, rotating down toward the sole at the toe. This factor and subsequent lameness may be misdiagnosed as founder (a common sequel to laminitis).

Laminitis, like white line disease, can result in hoof wall separation and coffin bone shift, but separation occurs within the attachment of the laminae; the sensitive laminae let loose from the insensitive laminae. In white line disease the separation occurs next to it instead. The main difference is that white line disease does not cause lameness unless it causes the coffin bone to drop, while laminitis is always painful. White line disease creates no pain as long as disintegration is confined to the horn tissue.

The cause of white line disease is still debated. Exposure to air seems to stop it, so anaerobic pathogens (yeast, fungi, or certain bacteria) are blamed. All the implicated microbes are usually found in soil — in almost every geographic region. Some researchers think these microbes are merely opportunistic invaders, taking up residence in a damaged hoof. This might explain the reason only one hoof on the horse or only one horse on a farm is affected. You rarely see white line disease unless some kind of mechanical stress has caused hoof wall separation.

A wet environment can soften and weaken the hoof at the white line, allowing microbes easier access into horn tissue. Urine and manure create chemical action that can dissolve and draw keratin from the horn cells. Wet feet hasten the breakdown process. Thus, environmental factors (wet climate, dirty conditions), mechanical stresses, and opportunistic microbes may combine to cause the disintegration of hoof horn.

White line disease can be treated by removing the diseased

hoof horn with clippers, grinding away all the remaining residue of affected horn, and treating the underlying tissue with a good fungicide. This treatment method may leave a large hole, so reconstructive shoeing is usually needed to support that part of the foot and prevent further separation of hoof from coffin bone. A patch of fiberglass or some other hoof-repair material can help stabilize the shoe while the foot grows out again.

Sunlight and air are good defenses against this disease, so most farriers and vets advise against sealing off the area. It's best to leave it open a few weeks before repairing the hole. They may use a broad-spectrum topical antibiotic or fungicide such as povidone iodine or bleach. Other products used are copper sulfate, formaldehyde, DMSO (dimethyl sulfoxide), pine tar, turpentine, gasoline, and merthiolate. Antifungal-impregnated hoof-repair materials are also useful. Early use of bleach or iodine can often stop white line disease before it spreads if the treatment is applied every day for a month and then every few days until new, healthy hoof horn has replaced the old, damaged horn.

How long it takes for destroyed horn to recover depends on how much hoof wall was lost. Advanced cases in which much of the wall is removed might take six months to a year for new horn to grow out. During that time the foot must be protected against reinfection. A small separation at the heel and quarters can be dug out and filled with medicated packing and the hoof shod to keep the packing in place. If the horse is kept in a dry environment and has his shoes reset regularly (replacing the medicated packing until the foot grows out), deterioration can be halted fairly quickly.

LAMINITIS

Laminitis disrupts attachments between the sensitive and insensitive laminae connecting the hoof capsule to the coffin bone. The inner part of this interface is nourished by tiny capillaries providing a steady flow of oxygen and nutrients to the laminae. The hoof's circulatory system has shunts that can channel blood directly from the arteries into the veins, bypassing the tiny capillaries. This unique arrangement keeps the feet from suffering frostbite in extremely cold weather (allowing blood to hurry through the foot without slowing down in the tiny network of capillaries, making the outer portion less vulnerable to freezing) but also makes the feet more vulnerable to laminitis.

Toxins in the blood from grain overload (and the resulting endotoxemia due to disrupted microbe population in the gut) or from systemic illness or uterine infection (retained placenta and "foaling founder") create chemical imbalances that adversely affect the shunts in the feet. The tiny capillaries in the laminae are deprived of blood — leading to cell death and blood clots. If enough laminae die, the attachment between the coffin bone and hoof wall comes apart and the bone begins to sink. The sinking of the coffin bone is called founder (like a sinking ship). The foot becomes deformed — the sole drops, the hoof wall spreads and develops rings and ridges, and the slope at the front of the foot becomes concave as the toe turns upward.

Laminitis may not end up as founder, depending on how much damage is done to the laminae. Because laminae at the toe of the front foot are under the greatest stress and have a comparatively more precarious blood supply, most cases of founder cause separation just at the toe. The coffin bone begins to separate from the hoof at the front tip and rotates toward the bottom of the sole, causing bruising in the sole and a flat or convex sole. The hoof wall at the toe is loose from its attachment and begins to peel from the coffin bone, turning upward. These separations in the hoof structure, loss of circulation, and tissue death all make the hoof more susceptible to infection.

Sometimes all the laminae are compromised and the coffin bone becomes completely detached (not just at the toe) and slides downward inside the hoof. This tears and destroys the areas crucial for normal hoof growth. The hoof may grow in deformed fashion or die completely and slough off — like a person losing a damaged fingernail.

During the first few hours (when the laminae are being damaged from lack of blood), the hooves are cool and the horse shows no symptoms. The blood is being diverted away from the capillary beds in the laminae and shunted back up the leg. One clue is an overly strong digital pulse. Then the acute and painful stage begins and can last up to seventy-two hours before the horse either recovers or goes into the final foundering stage.

A veterinarian should treat a horse in the earliest stages of laminitis to try to reverse the damage. Drugs may promote better capillary circulation and relieve pain. If laminae attachments are not already destroyed, the horse recovers. If changes are permanent, the problem becomes chronic, and the horse will need corrective trimming/shoeing.

If the coffin bone sinks or rotates, the horse needs long-term attention from a good farrier. Rotation is easier to deal with (and it's much easier to save the horse) than if the whole bone sinks. The traditional method for correcting a rotated coffin bone is to lower the heels until the frog bears weight, cutting back the toe as much as possible, to shift the weight from the damaged toe to the heels, which are usually less damaged. Cutting back the toe reduces breakover stress, keeping the hoof wall from being pulled farther away from the coffin bone at the toe. Lowering the heels also brings the coffin bone closer to its normal position.

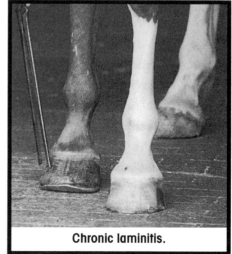
Chronic laminitis.

The farrier will usually

create a special shoe. A good farrier experienced in dealing with foundered horses should choose the best shoeing method for each case, combining or changing methods as the condition improves. Shoeing a horse with chronic founder is covered in the next chapter.

Diligent treatment and correction when a horse first develops laminitis can help damaged feet regain working soundness, though many cases require corrective shoeing for the rest of their lives. All too often the horse owner discovers the problem after the damage is done and the horse has entered the painful stage. The window for treating laminitis to prevent further damage is very short. Along with drugs (given by your vet) to reduce the pain, swelling, and inflammation, and increase blood flow, some kind of foot support may help prevent the damage created by weight-bearing. Weight should be spread over the entire foot, rather than concentrated on the hoof walls (where the compromised laminae can no longer hold the coffin bone in place). Help keep the laminae from tearing by letting the horse stand in deep bedding such as sawdust or sand (allowing the entire sole to take part of the weight) or filling the space inside the shoe with a rubber dental impression material.

NAVICULAR SYNDROME

Navicular problems commonly cause front foot lameness in domestic horses but are rarely seen in free-roaming individuals. Navicular syndrome may be a product of how we breed, use, and confine our horses. Horsemen used to think navicular syndrome was hereditary, but what is actually inherited is the conformation that can lead to it (small feet, upright shoulders and pasterns — anything that increases the effects of concussion).

The boat-shaped navicular bone is small and flat, lying deep inside the foot behind the coffin bone and short pastern bone. It provides a leverage point for the deep flexor tendon, serving as a bearing surface and shock absorber for that tendon and stabilizing its attachment to the coffin bone. The navicular bone keeps the coffin bone and short pastern bone properly aligned and helps decrease wear and tear on the coffin joint and flexor tendon.

The concussion of the foot on impact is transmitted through the coffin bone and navicular bone to the short pastern and on up the leg. The smaller the hoof in relation to the horse's weight, the greater the shock to the navicular bone and its associated tendons and ligaments. Upright pasterns can put more squeeze on the bone from the vertical pull of the deep flexor tendon against the vertical pressure from the short pastern bone. The ligaments holding the navicular bone in place are also stretched, straining their attachments and sometimes causing bone spurs.

What was earlier called "navicular disease" is a complex of several conditions that cause pain at the back of the foot. Often more than just the navicular bone is involved (or other tissues than the bone are causing the pain). Pain may come from the bone's suspensory ligaments, the coffin joint, deep digital flexor tendon, navicular bursa, or impaired blood supply to the navicular bone. Some horses with classic navicular lameness have normal navicular bones (on X-ray), and some horses whose X-rays are "bad" travel perfectly soundly. Knowing which area is hurting and why is crucial for proper treatment.

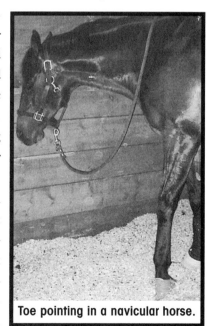

Toe pointing in a navicular horse.

Due to their conformation and use, some horses are more vulnerable to navicular syndrome than others. The highest incidence occurs in performance horses, usually seven to 14 years old. Quarter Horses and Thoroughbreds are affected more commonly than other breeds. Quarter Horses often have large bodies and small feet. Thoroughbreds seldom have navicular problems when young and racing, but in second careers as jumpers, eventers, etc., they are more at risk.

Horses in stalls are more vulnerable to navicular problems than horses at pasture. Standing in a stall puts constant pressure on feet and impairs their circulation. In most instances, navicular syndrome occurs only in the front feet (due to the extra stress and concussion they receive) but a hind foot may suffer if injured or punctured in the navicular region.

In early stages (which may encompass several years) the horse may be intermittently lame. He may improve with rest, but lameness recurs when he's used again. Lameness may be mild or just a gimpiness when he comes out of his stall. It may disappear with mild exercise but worsen when confinement follows strenuous exercise. Lameness may be present in both front feet or seem worse in one. Horsemen may not notice both fronts are sore until a veterinarian does a nerve block on the worst foot.

The first sign of lameness may be observed when the horse is turning or when the horse flinches while walking on gravel or rocks. He takes shorter, lighter steps, trying to keep weight off his front feet. He may point one front foot forward when standing still or stand with both fronts too far forward. The horseman might think he's foundered, but no heat is present in the hooves.

When the horse gallops, he has a short, choppy stride. He stumbles a lot because he tries to put his toe down first and not take weight on the heel, often stabbing his toes into the ground. He is less supple and agile; he may be reluctant to take a certain lead at the canter, or he may balk at jumps. The horse owner might think his horse is sore in the shoulders or going sour in his work because of his reluctance to perform. The horse may be short-strided and stiff when going downhill.

Over time, the foot changes shape. The horse's attempt to avoid frog pressure and heel weight causes the heels to rise and contract. The sole becomes more concave and the foot narrows across the quarters. If just one front foot is affected, it will be more contracted than the other. If unshod, the foot will be boxy, with high, contracted heels, a worn stubby toe, and a small frog well up off the ground. If the horse is shod, the toe of the shoe will show excessive wear.

A veterinarian can usually diagnose navicular syndrome based on the horse's history and clinical signs and may use X-rays and other methods [ultrasound, nuclear scintigraphy (bone scan), thermography, and MRI (magnetic resonance imaging)] to confirm the diagnosis. The horse will usually show pain when a hoof tester puts pressure across the heels, the central cleft of the frog to the toe, or the side cleft to the opposite heel. However, in some cases the horse won't respond to hoof testers. Veterinarians often use a local anesthesia to block the nerves that go to the navicular area. Unable to feel pain, the horse travels soundly. By anesthetizing certain areas of the lower leg, the vet can rule out or identify the many problems that make up navicular syndrome.

Treatment varies with each case. For best results, the vet must determine whether pain is coming from the tendons, ligaments, joints, cartilage, or the bone itself. Treatment may include corrective shoeing. Anti-inflammatory drugs may be used to ease the discomfort and enable the horse to use the foot normally again.

The sooner the problem can be treated and pain alleviated, the greater the horse's chances of recovery — even if you and your vet or farrier are not exactly sure what has caused the pain. If a horse shows signs of mild discomfort, don't postpone diagnosis by waiting for more obvious signs. By that time, the horse may have suffered more damage. Helping the horse use the foot normally again can often keep more damage from occurring.

A change in management can often relieve mild navicular

pain. If the problem is due to poor circulation or mild joint stiffness, exercise can help. The horse should be turned out or given light work. On the other hand, if the problem has been caused by excessive stress and concussion, the horse needs time off from hard work. Pasture turnout is helpful. About 90 percent of horses diagnosed with navicular syndrome can be helped with corrective shoeing (see Chapter 8). Regular trimming and shoeing at short intervals help maintain the best foot angle.

RINGBONE AND SIDEBONE

Ringbone is an osteoarthritis enlargement at the pastern or coffin joint; new bone growth is caused by injury to one of these joints.

The most common cause of ringbone is injury from strain or concussion during athletic activity or constant stress caused by poor conformation. A leg crooked at the fetlock joint (toeing in or out) puts greater stress on the pastern or coffin joint. Work increases this stress. Ringbone is more common in horses that compete in activities that call for sudden stops, turns, and other maneuvers.

Low ringbone is often more serious than high ringbone because it occurs beneath the coronary band inside the hoof, causing severe pain and lameness. Chronic low ringbone is often called buttress foot due to bulging of the coronary band at the front of the foot. The first sign of trouble (in either type of ringbone) is usually an intermittent lameness, heat, and tender swelling. As the condition becomes chronic, with new bone growth, the soft tissue around the joint becomes firm and cool. Pigeon-toed horses are more apt to develop ringbone on the outside of the joints; splay-footed horses develop it on the inside, due to stress on these areas from the crooked leg structure or from efforts to correct it.

A horse diagnosed with ringbone should be treated with anti-inflammatory drugs and rest. High ringbone sometimes heals with the pastern joint growing together. When the fusion is complete, the lameness disappears. Low ringbone usually creates a permanent problem. If treated early, ringbone can sometimes be managed for many years with careful use and special shoeing. However, the horse may eventually become chronically lame.

Sidebones are calcifications of cartilages on the sides of the foot. In a normal horse, these areas (on each side of the foot, back toward the heel and above the coronary band) are firm but moveable structures. They become sidebones if they turn to bone. Concussion is a major cause, especially in horses with upright pasterns. Splay-footed horses tend to get medial sidebones (inside of the foot) and pigeon-toed horses tend to get lateral (outside) sidebones, though it's not uncommon for sidebones to develop in both cartilage areas eventually.

Sidebones occur mainly in the front feet because they get the most concussion. Wire cuts or injuries that damage the cartilage may also cause sidebones. Poor shoeing can be a factor. Long heel calks increase concussion, and shoeing a horse off level may put more strain on one side. Foundered horses or horses with contracted heels are prone to sidebones because their feet are less able to handle concussion.

Sidebones may cause lameness only in the early stage when there is inflammation; most horses with healed, calcified sidebones have no lameness. If sidebones are causing lameness, the cartilage area will show heat and pain when pressed. The horse should be rested until the inflammation subsides and the bone is fully formed. Sometimes a sidebone will fracture because the calcified area is brittle and less flexible than normal cartilage. A fractured sidebone will cause sudden and severe lameness but will usually heal if the horse is rested.

CHAPTER 8

Corrective and Therapeutic Shoeing

UNDERSTANDING THE LIMITS OF CORRECTIVE SHOEING AND TRIMMING

The term "corrective shoeing" is often overused and misunderstood. It sometimes implies that the farrier can correct conformational faults of feet and legs. In reality, often very little can be done to change the way a horse is built. Trying to fix a horse's conformation problem via "corrective shoeing" will just put more stress on other parts of the limb.

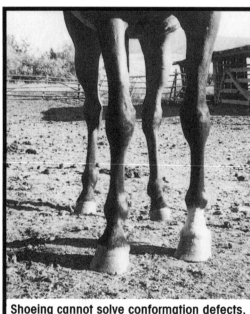

Shoeing cannot solve conformation defects.

No horse's limbs are perfectly symmetrical or perfectly aligned and balanced. A fine line exists between acceptable and poor conformation; it depends on how the horse is put together, how he handles his feet and legs, and how he is used. If he can manage to run, jump, cut cattle, or finish a hundred-mile endurance race without trouble and stay sound, you don't need to worry about "correcting" his faults. You can, however, make small corrections with each trimming or shoeing, to keep the feet as well balanced as possible to prevent limb interference.

Most farriers strive to keep the feet balanced and only in a few cases try "corrective" work. True corrections are generally done by trimming, not shoeing, because true corrections are only effective on foals.

CORRECTING A FOAL

Many small conformation problems can be corrected or kept from becoming more serious with regular, careful trimming when the horse is a foal. Often corrective trimming is simply a matter of balancing the foot. Without proper foot trimming, a leg slightly out of line may get worse as a foal grows. A crooked leg or a foot that toes in or out will produce uneven wear on the hoof, starting a vicious cycle — the more the foot wears unevenly, the more crooked the foot or leg becomes and the more uneven the foot wears.

The optimum time to attempt actual corrective trimming is the first four months of a foal's life and definitely no later than 12 months. After seven months, leg bones are not as malleable, and once bones are no longer growing, there's nothing you can do to correct a leg permanently.

However, overcorrection in young horses can be harmful. Lowering a foot too much on one side, for instance, may create pinching of the growth plate directly above it in the pastern or fetlock joint in a still-growing horse. Overcorrection also can cause prob-

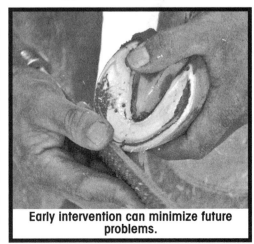

Early intervention can minimize future problems.

lems farther up the leg (whether the horse is young or mature) because changing the foot puts the rest of the leg off balance and violates that horse's conformational integrity. Corrections are best done frequently, in very small increments.

Also, keep in mind that many young foals toe out at first due to lack of muscle development. These foals generally straighten on their own as they grow and fill out. If you try to correct them, they will become crooked later due to interference with their bone growth.

A foal that toes in or out because of bone rotation at the fetlock joint or the entire leg can't be corrected with foot trimming. You must look at the whole leg to determine what should be done with a crooked foot. Knowing what types of deviations can be helped by trimming is very important because corrections may sometimes ultimately hinder or injure the horse.

INTERFERENCE PROBLEMS

Corrective trimming and shoeing can help problems such as forging or interfering. In these cases the farrier is trying not so much to change the foot or leg, but to enable the horse to travel more normally by minimizing the adverse effects caused by the extra weight of the shoe.

For a horse that interferes, this may mean trimming or shoeing so the foot starts its flight straighter (breaking over center rather than to the inside) to prevent hitting the opposite leg. If the foot is off level, a shim or half-rim shoe can raise the side of the foot that is too low. A shoe with inside rims and an open toe encourages proper breakover at the front. However, a square-toed shoe is often adequate to straighten the foot flight.

FORGING

If a horse forges, striking the front foot with the hind, use lighter shoes in front or hasten the breakover of the front feet by rolling the toe or using a rocker shoe or squaring the toe so the front foot is picked up faster. Front shoes also should be fitted closely at the heels so they are not struck or grabbed by the hind shoe and pulled off.

The hind foot can be shod in a way that shortens its stride, so the toe is less apt to meet the heel of a front foot. Some farriers use heel calks and a rocker toe on the hind feet to create more hock action and less forward movement. Sometimes the shoes on the hind feet are fitted so the toe of the shoe sits back (the toe of the hoof extends a little beyond the shoe) so the shoe itself does not hit the front heels.

STUMBLING

Stumbling is usually caused by something as simple as long feet (the horse is overdue for trimming) or shoeing, but it can be caused by something as serious as a brain injury or a neurological disease. Have your farrier or veterinarian examine a horse that stumbles frequently. You want to make sure the horse does not have West Nile Virus, EPM (equine protozoal myeloencephalitis), encephalitis, or some kind of spinal trauma that might make him uncoordinated. If neurological problems and illness are not the cause, a thorough lameness exam should be the next step. This can uncover or rule out a subtle lameness that might be putting the horse a little off balance. Some horses can still function fairly well with a slight lameness, but it makes them clumsier than normal. As soon as the lameness problem is resolved, the stumbling may stop.

Many horses that stumble are trying to land on their toes because of heel soreness. Toes that are too long and heels that are starting to run under may cause the heel soreness. Some horses shod the "normal" (traditional) way are still too long in the toes, even when freshly shod; the feet are not at a natural angle and balance (see Chapter Two). For example, when the horse would naturally have a 55-degree angle in the front feet, the farrier may trim and shoe the horse to create a 45- to 47-degree angle. The latter creates a much longer toe, and the horse may stumble.

Horses whose feet grow very fast might need trimming or shoeing a little more frequently to keep the toe short enough. Frequency, however, may depend on whether you can get the feet to balance. Many horses can go eight to ten weeks or even longer between shoeings and still be proportionately normal and well balanced.

You can roll the toe of a shoe to keep a horse from tripping, but how the foot is trimmed and balanced is actually more important than the type of shoe attached.

THERAPEUTIC SHOEING

Therapeutic shoeing refers to methods designed to help a hoof with a medical problem or some kind of functional impairment. Examples are glue-on shoes for horses whose feet can't hold nails because of thin or crumbling hoof walls or special shoes for bruised soles or foundered feet. If your horse has a lameness problem or injury, your farrier may use, or create, a special shoe to help resolve the problem or allow the foot to function more normally while it heals.

A regular metal shoe may be adapted for a specific purpose, such as clips added to stabilize a hoof crack, allowing it time to grow out. Or a shoe may have a rolled or rocker toe, or no toe at all, to make breakover very easy for a horse with laminitis. A horse with a tendon injury may need a very high heel to take tension and stress off the tendon. A horse with a puncture wound or some other type of foot infection may need a shoe with a removable plate over the sole to protect the sole yet allow daily treatment.

ARTHRITIC CONDITIONS

Therapeutic shoeing can often help joint problems, ringbone, and various other arthritic conditions. Though special shoes cannot cure any of these problems, certain shoeing innovations, such as shoes that make breakover easier, put less strain on the compromised joint as the horse moves, and help a horse travel more comfortably. Shortening the toe can help, and in some instances the farrier may raise the heels or use an egg bar shoe to provide more support to the rear of the foot.

BAR SHOES

Some shoes provide better support or protection for the foot. Bar shoes, for example, can provide extra support for certain parts of the foot. A bar shoe is often a continuous piece of steel or aluminum, with a "bar" connecting the heels. It can stabilize the hoof wall or relieve pressure on a corn or bruised sole. Originally used only as therapeutic aids for hoof and leg problems (such as navicular syndrome, sore heels, laminitis, hoof cracks, or bowed tendons), bar shoes are sometimes used on sound horses as well — to help correct or prevent a problem that might otherwise progress to unsoundness (such as underrun heels).

There are many types of bar shoes. A full bar shoe goes completely across the back, at the heels, to produce frog pressure if the bar is touching the frog (pressing in against the frog about a 1/4-inch when the shoe is nailed on), or to eliminate frog pressure if the bar is not touching the frog; the bar takes the weight instead of the frog. A half bar shoe extends partway across the heel from one of the branches to increase frog pressure and reduce concussion on the heels. An egg bar shoe is egg-shaped, with more heel support because it extends past the heels to provide a larger surface area than a traditional bar shoe. It diminishes concussion because it increases the foot's area of contact with the ground. A heart bar shoe applies selective pressure to the frog and is often

Bar shoe.

used on foundered horses to keep the coffin bone from rotating downward.

HOOF PADS

Many types of hoof pads can protect a sole from bruising (see Chapter 7), reduce concussion with better shock absorption, or compensate for hoof imbalance. Rim pads can reduce shock on the weight bearing walls while leaving the center open. Wedge pads are thicker at one end and can elevate the toe to reduce stress on certain frontal parts of the foot or lower leg, or elevate the heel and reduce stress on the rear support structures of the lower leg. Heel and frog supports can be used with bar shoes or egg bar shoes for treating coffin bone fractures, corns, and sole bruises. Pads with frog supports can relieve pressure on quarter cracks.

SHOEING THE CLUBFOOTED HORSE

A club foot has a hoof and pastern angle of more than 60 degrees, making the foot and pastern more upright than normal. The hoof is usually short and stumpy because it has a very short toe and a long (high) heel. The horse is walking on his toe, and the heel area does not get enough wear. This is caused by a shortening of the back tendon (which attaches to bones inside the hoof) and the muscles attached to that tendon above the knee. The hoof wall may have a steeper angle than the pastern; the foot angle is often broken rather than straight. Club feet may be due to genetics, nutrition, or injury. Often the condition affects just one front foot.

The contracted tendon/club foot is a common growth problem in young horses (up to six months of age). Contracted tendons, causing upright pasterns and a tiptoe stance, are often seen in foals with joint problems due to growing too fast. For instance, if one or both legs are sore from a joint problem, the foal may protect the joints by putting more weight on the toes; thus, the back tendons contract. The heel straightens and lengthens and the toe shortens. If discovered soon enough, this condition can be reversed by altering the foal's diet (eliminating the grain ration if he's growing too fast) and reducing stress on the legs so the damaged growth plates can heal.

A mild club foot may worsen if infrequently or improperly trimmed; by the time the young horse is two or three years old the problem becomes obvious. A club foot can also be due to injury if the horse favors his sore foot over time. This compensation can cause shortening and contracting of muscles and tendons in the sore leg, eventually making that foot more upright and stumpy.

The high heel and limited heel expansion usually cause a club foot to become contracted. The horse usually develops a rough gait and loss of agility due to improper foot angle. In many cases hoof horn grows faster at the heel than at the toe, accentuating the problem. Normal trimming intervals are inadequate for keeping the heels at proper length. That foot (primarily just the heels) may need to be trimmed more often. If not trimmed frequently, the extra heel growth causes the foot to become more upright between trimmings. Over time the abnormal foot angle causes misalignment and, sometimes, damage of the coffin bone. The foot becomes susceptible to sole bruising at the toe (most of the weight is carried on the toe). The sole is thinner under the front of the tipped-down coffin bone.

A club foot in a young horse can often be corrected or minimized as the horse grows, especially if noticed and treated early. Your veterinarian and/or farrier should deal with this problem because it may take surgery on the check ligament to change the angle of the coffin bone, as well as special trimming/shoeing, depending on the cause.

On an adult horse the heels of the club foot are often trimmed as much as possible from the point of the frog on back and a tapered wedge applied between the heels and the shoe to ease discomfort on the contracted tendon. Because the hoof and pastern are better aligned after trimming, the

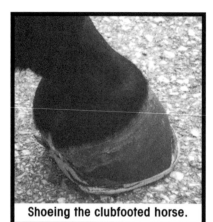
Shoeing the clubfooted horse.

tip of the coffin bone is not pressing so much on the sole, and the horse starts growing a better sole. He is able to stay sound, without the sole bruising and lameness that often accompany a club foot. However, the heel wedge is needed to keep him comfortable and to eliminate the extra pull on the check ligament and contracted tendons. If the club foot is caused by the horse favoring that leg as a response to pain somewhere else, then trimming the heels may actually worsen the club foot.

Often the best situation for an adult horse with a club foot is to leave that foot barefoot for a while, rasping the heels a little bit every few days and returning the hoof to a more normal angle and stride. Once the hoof is more normal, the horse can be reshod. Never try to "correct" a hoof angle problem such as a club foot all at once; you'll put too much stress on bones, tendons, and muscles.

Keep in mind that a club foot in a young horse is usually part of an upper leg problem; the horse may have a reason for altered stride and hoof angle, such as DOD (developmental orthopedic disease). It might be due to an OCD (osteochondritis dessicans), a lesion in a joint higher in the leg, for instance, or inflammation due to growth plates of the bones. The muscles tighten and the tendons contract because of pain response, pulling on the coffin bone in the foot and changing its angle. The foot becomes more upright as the deep digital flexor tendon contracts.

Sometimes, in an adult clubfooted horse, one front leg or shoulder is shorter than the other. If you stand in front of a club-footed horse (and he's standing straight, on level ground), the knee on the clubfooted side will be a 1/4- to a 1/2-inch higher than the knee on the normal side. If that horse isn't performing well and a flat pad is put under the shoe of the normal foot (thick enough to bring the knees level), the horse will perform evenly.

When dealing with this type of foot problem, evaluate the whole horse, especially the front end (or hind end). If a horse has asymmetrical front-end conformation, find a compromise in which you can trim/shoe the foot to enable the horse to move better and keep the foot angle from worsening without straining other structures by trying to change the horse's conformation. Many clubfooted horses are not lame, so you don't want to aggravate things by doing something drastic.

CONTRACTED FEET

(Common causes of contraction are discussed in chapter 7.)

In recent years, horsemen and farriers have learned that frog pressure is unnecessary for expansion of heels and quarters (some wild horses in desert environments never have frog pressure, yet still have healthy feet). Weight bearing alone forces the hoof wall outward. If the foot experiences proper weight bearing, heels won't contract.

With proper trimming and shoeing that allows heel expansion and weight bearing, most contracted feet will expand back to natural shape within a few shoeings. If the horse has navicular disease and his feet have contracted from disuse (reluctance to put weight on the heels because of increased

> ## AT A GLANCE
>
> Severity of a club foot is rated as follows:
>
> • Grade 1 is mildly upright with a hoof angle three to five degrees greater than that of the opposite foot.
>
> • Grade 2 has a hoof angle five to eight degrees greater than that of the opposite foot; the heel is long, with growth rings wider at the heel than at the toe.
>
> • Grade 3 has an angle more than eight degrees greater than that of the opposite foot; the front of hoof is dished (concave); and growth rings at the heel are twice as wide as at the toe.
>
> • Grade 4 has hoof angle of 80 degrees or more, putting the coronary band as high at the heel as it is at the toe; the front of the foot is very dished. The sole is so dropped it may actually be lower than the bearing surface of the hoof wall.

pain in that area), his feet can usually be helped by rolling the toe to encourage faster breakover and by protecting the frog so he will bear no weight in this most painful spot. If the pain can be decreased enough so the horse can bear weight more normally, the contracted heels tend to expand.

For years many people thought a full bar shoe would prevent heel expansion, but this is not necessarily true. A bar shoe can protect the frog and heel area but still allow hoof expansion — especially if the nails are placed so the heel and quarters can still move outward when the horse puts weight on the foot.

The best way to treat contracted heels is to identify the original cause and deal with it while enabling the foot to expand at the heel when bearing weight. It's what's done to the foot (rather than what's put on it) that matters. In most horses, balancing the foot and correcting any deviation from the normal foot angle will suffice, especially if the shoe can be fitted so it's slightly wider than the foot at the heel and quarters and the last nail can be placed ahead of the bend of the quarters, so as not to inhibit expansion.

UNDERRUN HEELS, UNEVEN HEELS, SHEARED HEELS

If the horse has a long toe and underrun heel, the same shoeing principles as used for contracted feet apply, along with shortening the toe as much as possible. More support can be given to the rear of the foot, such as with an egg bar shoe, until the heels remodel themselves for proper weight bearing. A rolled toe on a shoe that fits well back on the heel area tends to correct the problem. Some people try to leave as much heel as possible, but because the heel angle has put the ground surface of the heel so far forward, if you don't cut the heel off, you don't gain much ground surface to bring the heel rearward.

The goal of shoeing a horse with sheared heels (hoof symmetry distorted and one heel bearing most of the weight) is to restore balance in the foot and heels. A mild case can be corrected by trimming the longest heel and using a full bar shoe to stabilize the heel area. In many instances, removing the shoes, trimming the foot, and letting the horse go barefoot in a pasture or paddock with lots of room for exercise will eventually correct the condi-

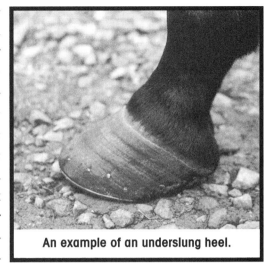

An example of an underslung heel.

tion. This method enables the foot to function more normally and redistributes the weight properly. Severe cases may need several trimmings and shoeings (with a full bar shoe) to restore foot balance and relieve the pain, using the horse's body weight (over time) to force the heel back into proper position and alignment.

NAVICULAR FEET

Some of the principles for shoeing the navicular horse have already been mentioned in the section on contracted feet. An egg bar shoe with rolled toe and raised heel can relieve pressure on the navicular area and ease breakover. Corrective shoeing can make many horses comfortable though some will benefit from "bute" on the days they are worked hard.

Maintaining proper foot balance is crucial for navicular horses. A good farrier often can help a navicular horse by matching the angle of the heels with the angle of the pastern and by providing adequate heel support. The toes should be short and rolled, and the hoof balanced from side to side and front to back.

How often a navicular horse is reshod is also important. Some horses with heel pain will do well for four to five weeks after being shod and then start to take shorter strides. They do better if shod every four to five weeks.

FOUNDERED FEET

Horses with foundered feet (chronic founder, in which hoof changes have already taken place) are often shod with a heart bar shoe; this type of shoe completely covers the heels, and the metal at each heel narrowly extends and bends inward to meet to create a cover for the central portion of the frog. A fair amount of frog should be visible all around the narrow protective bar. The toe of this shoe is usually rolled for ease of breakover. To know how much weight bearing should be taken by the bar over the frog, only a farrier who is experienced and successful in using this shoe for foundered horses should apply it. Pressure should never be exerted on the frog itself — merely support for the frog.

If not properly applied, this shoe can do more harm than good. And if the farrier or veterinarian does not understand how rapidly the foot can change, a perfectly applied heart bar shoe can be in such a bad position two weeks later that it can kill the coffin bone. Treating a foundered foot is an extremely labor-intensive process; a farrier must pay close attention to the progress, and many farriers don't have time to check on the horse every other day to make the necessary adjustments.

The heart bar shoe is designed to support the coffin bone (and leg bones above it) and should only be used after X-rays have shown how much the coffin bone has rotated to determine the amount of support needed. This will be continually changing as the coffin bone comes back toward normal position. Too much or too little support may worsen the situation.

In addition to the heart bar shoe, several other types of shoes can help the foundered foot. Glue-on shoes are often easiest for the horse because you don't want to drive nails into a painful hoof. Sole supports or heart bar shoes also can be glued on rather than nailed on because shoes may need to be changed often. Innovative support systems that hold up the hoof itself are probably a lot safer for many farriers and veterinarians to use than a heart bar shoe because the support system doesn't create pressure anywhere on the hoof. The amount of support will depend on the stage of founder and must be carefully monitored through the entire recovery process.

Shoes on a horse in early stages of founder are usually removed. Not wanting to concentrate weight on the hoof wall and laminae, most farriers and vets don't recommend shoeing a horse during the acute stage. The affected foot is supported by standing the horse in sand or by using Styrofoam or some kind

> ## AT A GLANCE
>
> Hoof care for foundered feet is aimed at:
>
> • removing forces placed on the compromised laminae by re-establishing weight bearing over the whole solar surface (inside the boundary of the shoe) of the coffin bone.
>
> • moving the breakover point back farther.
>
> • decreasing tension on the deep digital flexor tendon.

of impression material in the bottom of the foot to take the weight.

Before the horse is reshod, he must be past the acute stage and relatively comfortable — past the point of needing medication for pain. His feet should be stable, with no further changes on X-rays for at least 10 days to two weeks. By that time, he is in the chronic phase, and the farrier can deal with the problem mechanically by trying to correct the coffin bone's rotation. The vet or farrier may choose to use glue-on shoes to do this correction; this allows placement of the shoe wherever it is needed to change the weight bearing without having to nail it.

To know how to trim the foot and/or apply glue-on shoes at the proper angle to put the coffin bone in a better relationship with the ground surface, the farrier or veterinarian uses radiographs to show how much the coffin bone has rotated. The farrier or vet may not want the bone perfectly parallel to the ground, or it may sink farther under weight. The goal is to get better weight bearing on the whole bone rather than just the tip. A shoe that keeps breakover as far back as possible, behind the diseased laminae, often works best.

In chronic cases in which the coffin bone has rotated out of position, shoeing is also aimed at relieving compression of the sole and encouraging sole growth. The sole tissue in the toe becomes very thin where the bone puts pressure on it. Corrective shoeing can help a horse grow more sole in the toe. The foot is monitored with X-rays at each shoeing to make sure the horse is gaining sole and the coffin bone is moving toward proper position. Once a horse has foundered, the laminae are never as strong as in a healthy foot, so some kind of special shoeing to give him sole support or easy breakover may be necessary for the rest of his life.

GLUE-ON SHOES

Glue-on shoes can protect an injured foot or alter foot angle for medical purposes — giving extra frog support or sole support. In a foundered horse, for instance, the hoof wall is compromised; driving nails traumatizes and weakens the hoof even more. An innovative farrier, working with a veterinarian, can often create a special shoe to fit any purpose, designing it with whatever characteristics are needed for helping a particular hoof problem. Synthetic materials can even be used to reconstruct much of the hoof wall. Reconstruction and a glued-on shoe can support the foot while a new hoof grows.

Glue-on shoes are ideal for realigning the coffin bone in a foundered horse, especially if the foot does not have enough hoof wall or sole to accomplish this by traditional trimming/shoeing methods. A farrier may attach rails or wedges to the shoe to help raise the heels. Moving breakover back and raising the heels also decrease tension on the deep flexor tendon. The foot can leave the ground more easily (the weight doesn't have to move forward to break over), diminishing the pull of the tendon on the coffin bone at that point of the stride. Raising the heels after realigning the bone usually gives better results (in terms of comfort and less pain) and more normal hoof growth than simply realigning the coffin bone.

The final step in applying the glue-on shoe to a foundered foot is to fill the solar surface with impression material to support the whole foot and increase the weight bearing surface. This kind of shoe helps reduce pain, limits further damage to the laminae, and may facilitate better blood circulation — which in turn helps produce better sole and horn growth. Trimming the foot to realign the coffin bone tends to put the toe up off the shoe and often leaves a wedge-shaped air gap at the toe (between hoof and glue-on shoe) that must be filled with impression material.

Glue-on shoes should be reset every four to five weeks, with rails or wedges lowered at each reset — as the hoof wall grows out and the coffin bone gradually comes back to normal position. Usually the rails are only needed for the first few shoeings, but the glue-on shoes are continued until the hoof wall has regrown enough to maintain the alignment with trimming and conventional shoeing.

For other foot problems, repair material used for serious hoof cracks can be used for gluing on regular shoes. This material also holds up well when applied by itself to the bottom of the hoof wall as an extension. This can help a foal or young horse, for instance, when the base of support needs to be shifted for correcting a crooked leg, such as an angular limb deformity.

If a horse needs corrective or therapeutic shoeing, work with your farrier (and your veterinarian if the problem involves a medical situation). Do not attempt to tackle these challenges by yourself. You may end up being the person to continue the treatment or trimming, but your farrier and/or vet can get you started on the proper path.

CHAPTER 9

Pinpointing and Diagnosing Lameness in the Foot

A horse with a sore foot may appear obviously lame, but sometimes only carefully evaluating the horse's gait and closely examining the foot will reveal which foot is sore and where. If you are familiar with how a sound horse moves (the perfect regularity of gait and stride) at walk and trot, you can detect more readily when a horse is "off." Lameness is merely an alteration of gait as the horse tries to reduce the pain of weight bearing.

Although about 80 percent of all lameness problems are in the foot, some are located higher in the leg, and others are caused by back problems that lead to poor movement and more concussion. Hoof problems and back problems sometimes are so interrelated that determining where the problem originated is difficult. Often both problems need to be treated.

DETERMINING WHICH FOOT HURTS

You will be better able to identify which foot is lame if you have observed how your horse moves and listened to the sound of his hoofbeats on firm ground when he is healthy. This knowledge will enable you to recognize changes in the normal rhythm of gait and help you distinguish which leg is hitting the hardest (taking on extra weight) and which one the horse is trying to protect (coming to the ground more lightly).

Unless the horse is quite sore, the walk will not reveal much on casual observation. However, the trot is an ideal gait for spotting lameness. Diagonal legs strike the ground together. Because the trot is the most regular and symmetrical gait, the horse deviates more obviously as he compensates for a sore leg. Recognizing the lame leg at a canter or gallop is more difficult. As these are not symmetrical gaits, it's easier for a horse to minimize lameness, especially if he uses the lead that reduces strain on the sore leg.

AT A GLANCE

- The trot can reveal lameness, especially when the horse circles.

- Head-bobbing is a sign of lameness.

- Hind leg lameness is more difficult to detect.

A lame horse compensates for pain by getting off the sore leg as quickly as possible and changing his movement to redistribute his weight. These compensatory movements signal lameness. By watching closely, you can determine the sore leg. Head carriage is the most obvious clue because a horse uses his head and neck for balance, counteracting what is happening with the rest of his body. At the walk and canter, the horse's head bobs with each stride.

At a trot his head remains steady because he always has a diagonal pair of legs coming to the ground at the same time. Therefore, he doesn't need his head for balance. A horse that bobs his head at the trot is lame. He is trying to shift his weight off a sore foot or leg by balancing with his head and neck. Some horses will drop their heads a little at each stride, but it's an equal amount of drop as each foreleg comes to the ground — a normal and symmetrical little head bob rather than the significant drop when a certain foot comes to the ground.

To check for lameness, have someone lead the horse at a trot directly away from you and back again — with enough slack in the lead rope so the horse's head is free and you can see any hint of head-bobbing. Also watch from the side as the horse is trotted in front of something level, such as a fence. This reference point can help you see an asymmetrical head bob or a drop of the withers when the horse lands on the good leg. The horse can also be longed or led in a circle both directions. Some lamenesses are easier to see when the horse is turning.

Another way to determine which foot is sore is to lead the horse on hard ground and soft ground. Concussion on a hard surface will accentuate some types of lameness. A soft surface, one the foot sinks into — making the sole bear weight — will emphasize lameness involving the sole or tissues right above it. The way the horse stands at rest may also pinpoint which foot is lame — whether he tries to take weight off a foot by standing with the foot more forward of its usual position (front) or by resting it (hind).

FRONT LEG LAMENESS

In almost every front leg lameness, and even in a serious hind leg lameness, the horse's head bobs at the trot as he tries to take weight off the sore leg and put it more quickly on the good one. He lifts his head when the sore leg hits the ground and drops his head when the good foot lands. Some people misinterpret this because when humans are hurting, they tend to favor the side (foot or leg) that hurts.

If you have trouble watching a horse's head and feet at the same time, make it easier by saying "right, left, right, left" as each front foot hits the ground; once you have the rhythm firmly set, shift your vision to his head while you keep chanting. If his head rises each time you are saying "right" and drops each time you are saying "left," the soreness is in his right front limb. In a moderately lame horse you can see the horse's head move upward when the lame leg is on the ground; however, it's easier for most people to see the down movement. A horse with mild lameness usually doesn't make much of an up movement; the horse is just landing harder on the good leg. If you are riding the horse, you can feel the extra concussion when that good leg comes to the ground and also see his head bob.

A horse with equal pain in both front legs, such as from founder or navicular syndrome, will not bob his head much. He may hold it higher than normal as he tries to unburden his front legs and push his hind feet farther under himself to take more of the weight.

Sometimes having the horse travel in a circle locates the lameness. This puts more stress or pressure on the inside or outside of his feet or legs, causing him to compensate more noticeably. Sometimes, even when the vet can spot the lameness in a horse traveling in a line, he/she will want you to trot the horse in small circles to see if the opposite leg is involved as well.

The stress of trotting in circles differs from trotting in a line and can also help determine which front leg is lame. Generally, when you trot a horse in a circle, if the lame leg is on the inside, his lameness will be more pronounced because more stress is being placed on the inside leg. But some lamenesses on the outside leg worsen when circling. When a horse is circling to the left, for instance, more stress is placed on the outside of the left front leg and on the inside of the right front. Thus a circle may reveal more than trotting in a line.

HIND LEG LAMENESS

Compensation movements for a hind leg lameness are harder to detect. The horse may only bob his head for severe hind leg pain — and this may be misinterpreted as lameness in a front leg. A more reliable way to pinpoint hind leg lameness is to stand behind the horse as he is led directly away from you and to compare the up-and-down movement of his hips. If the pain occurs early in the stride as the lame foot takes weight, the rest of the stride will be quite shortened; the hip will pop up as the horse gets off that leg quickly. To evaluate hip movement better, it helps to imagine a big T on the back end of the horse, with the tail dividing the hind quarters in half and the horizontal top of the T connecting the points of the hips. As the horse moves, the rise and fall of the hips will thus be quite obvious as you envision this horizontal line.

A hind leg lameness is also fairly easily observed as the horse is trotted past you. Though detecting rear leg lameness (as compared to foreleg lameness) is more difficult because there's no head to balance movements, the principal is the same. The horse is protecting the lame leg by getting off it faster and putting increased force and downward movement on the good leg.

A hind leg lameness may affect how the horse carries his head, but the head carriage won't be pronounced unless the pain is severe enough for him to put more weight on the front legs. As he trots, his head may drop during the support phase of the diagonal foreleg, when the sore hind leg should be taking weight. If the right hind is sore, the horse's head will drop as the left front foot takes weight. If you are only looking at his head carriage, however, and not evaluating the hip movement as well, you might mistakenly assume he is lame in the right front.

You need to look for downward movement of the good hind leg. Although you can watch the hip or the point of the tail head for clues, the whole hindquarter movement is the biggest clue. You can see the up-and-down movement of the rear end, like a bouncing beach ball, and if you can time the exaggerated downward movement of the rear end with the good leg, you'll know the horse is lame on the other leg.

If you watch the horse from the side as he's trotting past, you can also see the other gait changes that indicate lameness, such as shortening stride. With most front leg lamenesses, the horse doesn't shorten his stride much, and if he does, it's not easy to detect by watching the horse trot (head movement is a better clue.) But stride length is the best clue for detecting lameness in the hind legs. Rear leg lameness, even if it's mild, usually results in a shorter stride on the hurt leg.

Thus, look for increased impact (downward force) on the good leg and shorter stride on the lame leg. These are very obvious if the horse's movements are videotaped and later replayed in slow motion. A veterinarian may use this method to detect a subtle hind leg lameness. It can be hard to see at regular speed as the horse is trotting, but you can compare how closely the rear foot is coming to the front foot (left side versus right side). The more severe the lameness, the shorter the stride will be on the lame leg.

Trotting in circles may reveal a rear leg lameness, not so much by a shortened stride length (since the inside leg always takes a shorter stride when circling), but by concussion changes. Most lameness exams are done on hard ground, making it easier to see and hear effects of concussion. Impact accentuates pain. A few lamenesses involving ligament and support structures may worsen when a horse travels on soft ground or in deep footing, but these types of lamenesses are more easily seen on a smooth, hard surface because concussion affects these problems, too.

PINPOINTING THE SORENESS

Once you determine which leg is sore, the next step is to locate the problem's origin. If a horse is reluctant to put full weight on a leg, the first place to look is the foot. The problem may be as simple as a rock caught in the foot or wedged in the shoe. Some indication of trauma or infection, such as a puncture or an advanced case of thrush may be present. If nothing is obvious, a hoof tester might locate a sore area, indicating a bruise or abscess under the sole.

If the bottom of the foot seems fine, check for heat in the hoof wall. Compare it to the temperature of the other feet. Feel both fronts, or both hinds. Check for pain around the coronary band by squeezing the coronet and the heels with your hands. Compare the digital pulse of both feet by pressing your fingers against the artery that runs under either side of the fetlock joint. If you are still at a loss, check the leg from top to bottom for heat and swelling (compare it to the sound leg). Even subtle changes can be detected by comparing legs. Also compare the joints for thickness and swelling, heat, or sensitivity. Your hands can often give clues that the eyes can miss, and the horse's reaction to your touch can also indicate soreness.

If you check the feet and legs daily — during grooming, before and after a ride or workout, and the next day after a hard workout — you can discover some problems in their early stages. Checking the pulses of the legs is also helpful when you are trying to pinpoint a lameness. The prominent artery that goes over the back of the sesamoid bones is easy to feel. A lame horse may have an increased pulse in the sore leg, which can indicate a problem, such as a sole abscess or infection, in the lower leg or foot.

Your farrier or vet may also locate pain using manipulation tests. For example, a flexion test may show a sore fetlock joint. The leg is flexed or extended and then the horse is trotted off and observed for signs of lameness. The manipulation stresses the joint and makes the lameness easier to see. It may also make the horse resist the manipulation.

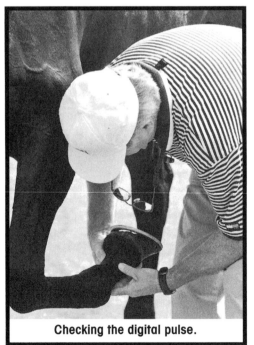
Checking the digital pulse.

To test for navicular pain, the front leg is extended with the toe lifted and held up for a minute or more. Then the horse is immediately trotted. Limping on the tested leg for the first fifteen yards usually indicates a problem with one or more of the joints in his lower leg (fetlock, pastern, or coffin), which could mean inflammation in the coffin and navicular joints. Only about 10 percent of horses with navicular syndrome fail to react to this flexion test, and it's a good way to test for heel pain.

Once you locate the area of soreness in a leg, the next step is to determine the cause (injury or infection) and how to treat it. Your vet may need to help with the diagnosis and almost always should advise on the most effective treatment unless it's some-

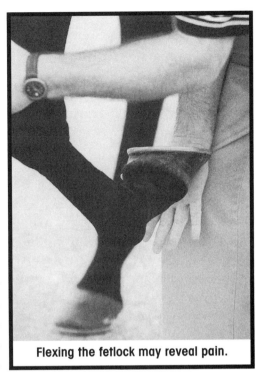

Flexing the fetlock may reveal pain.

thing simple such as a rock caught in a shoe.

If your vet or farrier cannot pinpoint the problem with simple examination (checking for heat, pain, and swelling, or using flexion tests), then he may need some other diagnostic tool, such as nerve blocks or some more sophisticated tests such as a bone scan. The diagnosis becomes more complex if multiple limbs are involved. Many bilateral lameness problems may affect both fronts or both hinds, and occasionally a horse is lame in all four legs. Sometimes lameness is actually a secondary problem (if a horse has a neurological problem, such as EPM — equine protozoal myeloencephalitis), so consult your vet to help track down the true cause.

USING A HOOF TESTER

Your vet or farrier may use a hoof tester to pinpoint the area of soreness. Someone who looks at lame horses all the time is more able to tell if the horse's response to the pressure is normal.

The typical hoof tester has large semi-circular tongs for gripping the foot and parallel handles with a pinch stop to protect fingers. The design amplifies the strength of the grip so pressure can be put on the sensitive structures beneath the hard surfaces of the wall and sole. Making a sound horse flinch usually takes a lot of force, while only moderate pressure on an injured, bruised, or inflamed area will cause the horse to flinch or pull away his hoof.

To learn how to use a hoof tester, practice on a number of horses, sound and lame. To check the hoof thoroughly, start in the same area each time and systematically check every part of the foot from the outer edges to the center of the frog. With any horse you check, first determine his sensitivity to ordinary pressure. Some horses are more stoic; it takes more pressure to get them to respond. Place one prong of the tester in the angle of the sole and wall, near the heel, and squeeze — gradually squeezing harder until he flinches. This will help you judge his subsequent reactions to pressure on other areas, keeping in mind that if the heel you squeezed first is the sore one, his reaction will be less in other areas.

Mike Williams (owner of Brand W Horseshoeing Supply, Livingston, Montana) created a hoof tester with a spring-loaded calibration device to show exactly how much pressure is exerted. This very useful device gives a standard and objective measure of the horse's soreness.

The first test squeeze indicates how much pressure is necessary to make the horse flinch. If it takes less in another spot, you'll know you hit a sore place, provided the same amount of pressure has been carefully applied to each area. If a certain area seems sensitive, mark that spot with chalk or a pen and complete your full examination (in case it's not the only problem area), then retest the sensitive spot to make sure the horse's first reaction was not caused by something other than pain.

Check the perimeter of the sole, moving the tester in small increments (about 3/4-inch at a time) around the foot. Keep the inside prong close to the white line. A flinch in this general area could mean a shoe nail driven too close to the quick or an infection that has worked up through the white line. Then make a second circle inside the white line, about halfway between it and the frog to check the middle area of the sole. Sore spots anywhere around this circle could mean a stone bruise, hoof abscess, puncture wound, a coffin bone fracture, or laminitis.

A common place for stone bruising is between the toe and point of the frog. Squeeze along the bars of the hoof to check for possible corns (bruising at the angle between hoof wall and bars) or a puncture, and along the entire length of the frog on both sides. Pain here could indicate a bruise, deep thrush, or a puncture — which can be hard to see because of the frog's spongy nature.

Pain response in the midline of the frog could mean a puncture or coffin bone fracture. Pain only in the central part means pain around the navicular bone. The bone may or may not be inflamed; the problem could be the bursa, tendons or ligaments supporting the bone, or even the digital cushion. Finally, check for sensitivity across the heels by pressing with the tester tips below the hairline of the heel bulbs. Pain in this area could indicate laminitis, a fractured coffin bone, sheared heels, or any other type of heel pain — such as a bruise, abscess, imbedded nail, or even a strain of the heel ligament.

The challenge in using hoof testers is that a horse with a subtle foot soreness may not always react. His feet ache a little, but unless you put a lot of pressure on the sole you can't make him respond to hoof testers. By the same token, you can take a perfectly sound horse and make him respond to hoof testers if you squeeze hard enough. Learning to use hoof testers is an art you must master to accurately detect lameness.

GLOSSARY

Abscess — A localized pocket of pus in damaged, infected tissue.

Arthritis — Inflammation of a joint.

Articular — Pertaining to a joint surface.

Balance — In a balanced foot the forces on the hoof are all equal, with no extra stresses.

Bars — Bracing structures on the bottom of the foot at each side of the frog, formed by the hoof wall turning inward at the heels.

Bar shoe — Shoe with bar across the back to add or reduce weight bearing on certain parts of the foot.

Base narrow — Limbs are closer together at the feet than at the tops of the legs.

Base wide — Limbs are farther apart at the feet than at the tops of the legs.

Blow out — Horizontal hoof crack.

Borium — Tungsten carbide "hard-surfacing" material (harder than steel) added to a shoe to increase traction or extend the life of a shoe.

Bowed tendon — Inflammation and damage in a flexor tendon, giving it a swollen and bulging appearance.

Breakover — Act of lifting the foot from the ground heel first, rolling over the toe. The breakover point is the last part of the hoof to leave the ground.

Bursa — Small fluid-filled sac that prevents friction between moving parts, such as between a bone and a tendon.

Buttress foot — Chronic low ringbone with bulging of the coronary band at the front of the foot.

Calks — Extra material on a shoe, at toe or heels, to add traction.

Canker — Infectious condition of sole or frog that results in abnormal growth of soft horn.

Cannon bone — Long bone between the knee (or hock) and fetlock joint.

Cartilage — Firm connective tissue; in a young, growing horse it serves as a precursor to bone.

Chestnut — Horny growth on the inside of the upper legs.

Clinch cutter — Tool to cut the nail clinches when removing a shoe.

Clinching tool — Tool to bend the nail tip tightly against the hoof wall after pounding the nail head firmly into the shoe.

Clips — Extra material on the shoe (alongside the hoof) to help hold the shoe in place.

Club foot — Stumpy hoof in which the heel grows long and the front portion of the foot is too upright.

Coffin bone (third phalanx, pedal bone) — The large bone within the foot, lying between the short pastern bone and the sole.

Coffin joint — Joint between the short pastern bone, coffin bone, and navicular bone.

Concussion — Stress of impact when the foot hits the ground.

Conformation — Shape and structure of the body and its various parts.

Contracted heels — Narrow heels, with bars too close together.

Corium — The living lining inside the hoof wall that produces the hoof horn.

Corn — A bruise on the bottom of the foot at the angle of the bars (where the bar meets the hoof wall).

Coronary band — The top portion of the hoof wall, adjoining the skin and hair of the leg, containing horn-growing cells that produce the horn tubules that make up the hoof wall.

Digital cushion — The dense, spongy tissue in the rear half of the foot, above the frog.

Digital pulse — Pulse taken at the artery that runs under the side of the fetlock joint.

Dished toe — The front of the foot is not a straight line but curved, with a tendency to curl up at the toe; the foot has spread forward at the toe.

Dropped sole — Instead of being concave, the sole bulges downward and is easily bruised and injured.

Dub off — Wear off (the toe).

Duckett's dot — Indentation in the frog, near the point of the frog.

Edema — Swelling (fluid in the tissues).

Egg bar shoe — Egg-shaped bar shoe, to provide additional support for the heel area.

Ergot — Small, horny tissue at the rear of the fetlock joint, usually covered with fetlock hair.

Exfoliation — Self-trimming process of the sole; the old, dead tissue continually flakes away.

Extensor tendon — Tendon that straightens a joint.

Feral — Domestic animal gone wild.

Fetlock joint — Joint between the cannon bone and long pastern bone.

Flare — The non-symmetrical spread outside of the ground surface of an unbalanced foot.

Flat-footed — Foot with a sole that is flat and level with the ground instead of concave.

Flexion test — Manipulation of a joint to make a lameness easier to detect.

Flexor tendon — Tendon that bends a joint.

Foot flight — Path a foot takes when taking a stride.

Forging — When a hind foot strikes the heel or sole of a front foot as the horse moves.

Founder — Sinking of the coffin bone and resultant hoof deformities following a severe case of laminitis.

Four-point trim — Removing the ground surfaces between the four points of contact or pillars of support (heels and each side of the toe) to mimic the natural barefoot hoof.

Frog — V-shaped cushion of rubbery material on the bottom of the foot (rear two-thirds) at the middle of the sole.

Gravel infection — Infection inside the foot that enters at the white line and travels upward to break out at the heel or coronary band.

Heel — Rear portion of the hoof.

Heel bulbs — Rounded portions at each side of the rear of the foot, above the coronary band.

Hoof angle ratio — Relative slope of the angle at the front of the hoof versus the slope of the heel.

Hoof crack — A split in the hoof wall.

Hoof knife — Farrier's tool to trim the sole.

Hoof pad — Covering that protects the sole.

Hoof pick — Curved tool to clean the feet.

Hoof testers — Tool with large tongs for gripping the foot and putting pressure on specific locations to check for pain response.

Hoof wall — Horny outer covering of the hoof.

Horn — Hard outer surface of the foot and sole.

Horn tubules — Tiny tubes that make up the outer hoof wall.

Insensitive laminae — Inner tissues of the hoof wall that interlace with the sensitive laminae that contain blood and nerves.

Interference — Striking one foot or leg against the opposite one.

Intra articular — Inside a joint.

Joint — Juncture between two or more bones.

Joint capsule — Sac containing lubricating fluid that encloses the portions of bones that make up a joint,.

Keratin — Protein that makes up the major portion of hoof horn, hair, and skin.

Knee — Joint between upper and lower portions of the foreleg.

Laminae — Interlocking tiny folds of tissue that bind the hoof wall to the foot.

Laminitis — Inflammation of the laminae; blood supply is interrupted, causing breakdown of the bond between the coffin bone and the hoof wall.

Lateral cartilage — Firm area of cartilage protruding up and back from the wing of the coffin bone on the outside (lateral) edge of the foot.

Ligament — Connective tissue holding bones together.

Long pastern bone (first phalanx) — Bone between the fetlock joint and short pastern bone.

Medial cartilage — Firm area of cartilage protruding up and back from the wing of the coffin bone on the inside (medial) edge of the foot.

Nailbound — Discomfort due to the shoe's being too tightly nailed to the hoof.

Navicular bone — Small bone in the foot, lying behind the coffin bone.

Navicular syndrome — Degeneration of the navicular bone and/or its support structures.

Nippers — Tool used for trimming the hoof wall.

Over-reaching — Hind foot comes to the ground farther forward than the front foot that was just picked up. This term is sometimes used to describe forging.

Over-extension — Excessive extension (straightening) of a joint.

Paddling — Swinging the feet outward as they are picked up; a common action in pigeon-toed horses.

Pastern — Area between fetlock joint and foot.

Pastern joint — Joint between first phalanx (long pastern bone) and second phalanx (short pastern bone).

Periople — Narrow strip at the top of the hoof, similar to the cuticle on a human fingernail.

Periosteum — Lining around a bone.

Phalanx — Any of the three "finger" bones of the horse's foot: long pastern bone (first phalanx); short pastern bone (second phalanx); coffin bone (third phalanx).

Pigeon-toed — Toes turning inward rather than facing forward; toes closer together than the fetlock joints.

Plantar cushion (See digital cushion.)

Plate shoe — Shoe with a flat ground surface; no buildup at heel or toe.

Polo plates — Rim shoes with higher inside rim to give traction.

Poultice — Soaking material that helps draw out infection.

Quarter — Rear portion of hoof, from the widest point to the heel.

Quick — Living tissue just inside the hoof wall or sole.

Quicked nail — Nail that pricks the sensitive tissues.

Rasp — Tool to trim and smooth the hoof after excess horn has been cut away with hoof nippers (cutters).

Rim shoe — Shoe with a groove running around the entire ground surface.

Ringbone — Extra bone growth at or near the pastern or coffin joint.

Rocker toe — Shoe with toe curved upward even more than a rolled toe.

Rolled toe — Shoe with toe rolled upward to shorten the toe and make easier breakover for the foot.

Seedy toe — Separation at the bottom of the foot at the white line.

Sensitive frog — Digital cushion, directly above the frog.

Sensitive laminae — Tiny fingers of tissue at the outside portion of the sensitive inner tissues of the hoof, interlocking with the insensitive laminae of the hoof wall.

Sesamoid bones — Pair of small bones at the rear of the fetlock joint.

Sheared heels — One heel bulb is higher than the other and the tissue between them is torn and damaged.

Short pastern bone (second phalanx) — Bone between the long pastern bone and the coffin bone.

Sidebone — Calcified cartilage at the side of the foot above and below the coronary band.

Sole — Horny tissue on the bottom of the foot.

Splay footed — Toes pointing outward (feet wider apart than the fetlock joints).

Splint — Bony enlargement on the splint bone/cannon bone (along the upper two-thirds of the cannon bone).

Sticker — Calk used only on the outside heel of a hind shoe.

Stone bruise — Bruised sole.

Stratum tectorium — Outer surface of the hoof wall.

Stride — Length of each step.

Studs — Calks that can be driven or screwed into the shoe.

Sulcus (sulci) — Groove at the side of the frog or down its center.

Suspensory ligament — Ligament that supports a bone, such as the fetlock joint.

Tendon — Connective tissue attaching muscle to bone.

Therapeutic shoeing — Using a special shoe to treat a hoof with a medical problem or functional impairment.

Thrush — Infection in the clefts of the frog.

Toe — Front part of the hoof or shoe.

Toe grab — Protrusion across the toe of a shoe's ground surface, to aid traction.

Underrun heels (underslung) — Heels are lower than normal, with an angle putting the ground surface too far forward.

Unsoundness — Any condition that impairs the usefulness of the horse.

White line — Light-colored line at the ground surface of the foot dividing the hoof wall from the sole.

White line disease — Disintegration of inner portion of the hoof wall, starting at the white line (usually due to a separation there) and moving upward.

Wide web shoe — Shoe with bearing surface wider than normal.

Winging — Swinging the foot inward as it leaves the ground, a common action in splay-footed horses.

RECOMMENDED READINGS

Books:

Adams, OR. *Lameness in Horses*. Philadelphia: Lea & Febiger, first edition 1962; third edition 1974.

Brega, Julie. *The Horse: The Foot, Shoeing & Lameness*. London: JA Allen, 1995.

Hill, C. and Klemish, R. *Maximum Hoof Power*. New York: Howell Book House, 1994.

Jackson, Jaime. *Horse Owners Guide to Natural Hoof Care*. Harrison, AZ: Star Ridge Publishing, 1999.

Jurga, Fran. *Understanding the Equine Foot*. Lexington, KY: Eclipse Press, 1998.

King, C. and Mansmann, R. *Equine Lameness*. Grand Prairie, Texas: Equine Research Inc., 1997.

Rooney, James R. *The Lame Horse* (updated and expanded). Neenah, WI: Russell Meerdink Co., 1997.

Sellnow, Les. *Understanding Equine Lameness*, Lexington, KY: Eclipse Press, 1998.

Stashak, TS. *Adams' Lameness in Horses*, fifth edition, Philadelphia: Lea & Febiger, 2002.

Stashak, TS and Hill, C. *Horseowner's Guide to Lameness*. Baltimore: Williams & Wilkins, 1995.

Magazines:

American Farriers Journal, P.O. Box 624, Brookfield, WI 53008-0624. www.americanfarriers.com

Hoofcare & Lameness: The Journal of Equine Foot Science, P.O. Box 6600, Gloucester, MA 01930-4167. www.hoofcare.com

PHOTO CREDITS

CHAPTER ONE
Robin Peterson, 11, 12; Anne M. Eberhardt, 14, 17.

CHAPTER TWO
Anne M. Eberhardt, 26, 27; Chris Pollitt, 28; Robin Peterson, 31; Mitch Taylor, 34.

CHAPTER THREE
Janis Tremper, 36; Anne M. Eberhardt, 40, 42.

CHAPTER FOUR
Heather Smith Thomas, 47, 50; Anne M. Eberhardt, 52, 57; H.F. Woodall, 55; Janis Tremper, 57.

CHAPTER FIVE
The Horse magazine, 64; Heather Smith Thomas, 66, 67.

CHAPTER SIX
Kim/Kari Baker, 72; Anne M. Eberhardt, 74; *The Horse* magazine, 79.

CHAPTER SEVEN
H.F. Woodall, 80; Heather Smith Thomas, 87, 104, 105; Anne M, Eberhardt, 92, 95, 96, 100, 101, 111, 115; Janis Tremper, 96, 97, 98, 99; Earl Gaughen, 102; Taryn Sukikowski, 102; Ric R. Redden, 102; Amy Rucker, 108; Julie Grohs, 117.

CHAPTER EIGHT
Heather Smith Thomas, 122; Anne M. Eberhardt, 123, 127; Steve O'Grady, 130, 133.

CHAPTER NINE
Anne M. Eberhardt, 144, 145.

COVER
Dusty Perrin

ACKNOWLEDGMENTS

This book should probably be dedicated to my 4-H leader Jerry Ravndal, a horse breeder and farrier who helped me get started shoeing my own horses when I was a teenager. In 1962 I purchased the first edition of Dr. O.R. Adams' book *Lameness in Horses* and it became my shoeing "bible."

I want to thank some of the people I've interviewed or talked with in more recent years (for articles on hoof health and foot care), whose thoughts and comments helped shape parts of this book. These people include Tia Nelson, farrier and veterinarian in Helena, Montana; Jaime Jackson, former farrier in Arizona and author of books on natural foot care; Robert Schneider, DVM, MS, professor of equine orthopedic surgery at Washington State University; Stephen O'Grady, BVSc, MRCVS, veterinarian and farrier in Virginia; Barney Fleming, DVM, Deming, New Mexico; Wayne McIlwraith, DVM, MS, PhD, professor of surgery, Colorado State University; David McCarroll, DVM, Goldsby, Oklahoma; William H. McCormick, VMD, Middleburg, Virginia; Brendon W. Furlong, MVD, Oldwich, New Jersey; Richard Galley, DVM, Willow Park, Texas; John Tisdale, DVM, Andalusia, Alabama; Bradley Jackman, DVM, Oakdale, California; Scott Morrison, DVM, Lexington, Kentucky; Bill Moyer, DVM, large animal medicine and surgery, Texas A&M University.

ABOUT THE AUTHOR

Heather Smith Thomas started shoeing the family ranch horses in 1958 when she was 14, after watching her dad, Don Smith, do the shoeing. During her early years of shoeing, her 4-H leader Jerry Ravndal (a horse breeder and farrier) gave her many tips. During the past 47 years, she has shod all her ranch horses and has been intensely interested in health and care of their feet as the soundness of these horses has been vital to her ranching operation in the rugged mountains of Idaho. She and her husband Lynn have been raising beef cattle and horses since 1966.

During the 1970s, she took time out occasionally from ranch work to do some endurance riding. In 1976 she sought advice on shoeing a horse she was campaigning, devising a metal plate to cover the hole in his sole from an abscessed stone bruise that had to be opened to drain. That horse finished the competitive season and chased cows between rides.

While still in high school, she started writing about horses and cattle; her stories and articles helped pay her way through college at the University of Puget Sound. Her first book, *A Horse in Your Life*, was published in 1966. Since then she has written more than 7,000 articles for horse and livestock publications and has published 18 books, including *Care & Management of Horses* (Eclipse Press, 2004).